It Wasn't Supposed to End 1 years in the making. After carin_ her mother for 22 years, Reese spent the next five years documenting the relationship and passing of her second husband, the love of her life, and her always loving and ever charming mother–both of whom were dying at the same time.

Each day challenged Reese's strength, and at times her patience, yet each day was an opportunity to laugh with her quick-witted husband and wickedly funny mother while finding ways to honor the love they shared.

Once the pain of loss began to lift, Reese realized she was no longer a caregiver, so she set out to redefine her purpose in life. Using her business planning skills, she created a process to transform the pain in her life to a future full of meaning.

Hers is a love story. Her process to redefine purpose provides a path out of grief. Both are within the cover of this book.

It wasn't supposed to end this way

JR Publishers
California State University, Fullerton
Ruby Gerontology Center-7
Fullerton, 92835-6870

ISBN-13: 978-0692864630
ISBN-10: 0692864636

Cover Design by Veronica Michalowski
Front cover photograph by Otnaydur/Shutterstock

This book is dedicated to my loving husband,
Robert Canady,
and my ever delightful mother, Miss Elma.

There are so many wonderful people who helped this story come alive. I offer my thanks to Jill Johnson-Young and Dr. Tony Bell for reviewing my work and to Kenda Kellawan-Shafer for hosting my grief workshops.

Thanks to my many partners in writing and reviewing: Donna Judd, Mary Ellen Cummings, Muriel Bergman, Keni Cox, Kitty Baier, Ron Baesler, Judy Smith, Juanita Driskell, and the many class members who listened to me read my work and provided me with invaluable feedback. Fritz Von Coelln patiently helped me format and get this book into print, for which I will be eternally grateful.

To Jane Rollingson, special thanks for reading this story from the perspective of a grassroots leader in hospice care. I am so pleased you saw the love in this story.

A heartfelt thank you to Bob's sister, Hilda Harris, who helped me capture the 1930's essence of Screven, Georgia—the small community that nurtured Bob and his two sisters.

A special thank you to Veronica Michalowski who read my work, provided excellent coaching, and is the talented artist who designed my cover. To my dear friend, Annette Gilzene, Bob's former Executive Assistant, thank you for reading this book, giving me your feedback and excellent guidance.

I offer heartfelt thanks to my literary muse and editor, Mr. Henry Smith, who has been supportive from the first chapter of this book. Thank you, Hank.

There are those who helped care for both Bob and Miss Elma. Keli Kaye came every chemo week to help us manage the challenges that faced us. Ron Canady flew from Florida to California to lovingly entertain his father, and to take over the kitchen with a talent far beyond ours. And there were many caregivers who watched over Mother giving me the opportunity to be a daughter. Zena, May and Ruth helped the very last few days of Mother's life. I will forever be grateful to the love and care each caregiver shared with us.

I could not close without extending gratitude to two physicians on my husband and my mother's teams: Drs. Martin Bae and Donald Abrahm. Dr. Abrahm, thank you for supporting me through the loss of two husbands and my mother. Dr. Bae, thank you for "being there" on weekends, and even the middle of the night. I will never forget your kindness as you sat with us that last evening in ICU. I always knew you would be there, and I always counted on you.

It takes a community to help someone get through dying, the last task of life. It also takes a community to "birth" a book. I am very lucky to have such a community.

Table of Contents

Introduction

Please, join me on my journey. It is a world of love, of loss, and of hope.

Why did I write this book? It is a love story I felt compelled to write since Death left me behind on this earth. I cared for two husbands and a mother for most of twenty-two years. I was forced to give up consulting—my passion—due to health problems. I had no hobbies that inspired me. As a reader, you will walk with me through the loss of my husband and my mother, the two most important people in my life, both dying at the same time. After their deaths, surviving meant reinventing my life. So I did.

I began to write stories until one story after another merged into a book. When I finished each chapter, it was as though my brain chemistry had a party, and the high lasted for days. It was then that the loneliness began to fade.

In June of 2012, the AARP Bulletin printed my story entitled, "What I Know About Starting Over." My website was suddenly flooded with visits.

A few months later, I was contacted by a hospice company in Santa Maria, California, which led to a presentation on managing grief at a hospice seminar. I shared my writings, then took those experiencing grief through a process to help them redefine their purpose after loss.

The responses surprised and overwhelmed me— those going through loss said my writings were of great help to them. The writings seemed to give them a sense of direction to grow beyond their current suffering. The hospice counselors agreed.

More importantly, after experiencing the process, many of the participants stated openly they finally had hope.

One declared, "If you can do it, Jeanette, I can do it, so I am going back to school!"

Other hospice counselors began to use my stories to train hospice staff. One therapist encouraged me to continue to write and publish since she believed others would benefit from my writings. These stories are now the chapters of this book. I hope you find them helpful.

After the chapters of this memoir, you will find the *Letter to my Readers*. In it, I outline a simple guide to help process one's grief, but it does not stop at processing. I have outlined the steps that help us redefine or reconnect to our purpose. It is this resolve that pulls us through our pain. If you have or are experiencing grief, you may find this letter helpful.

There are many causes of grief or a sense of loss. Losing a loved one is particularly painful, but the loss of a career or job, the loss of health, the empty nest syndrome— all these things and more can cause a deep reevaluation of life as one repurposes for the future. Each loss challenges our core being. Each time we have the option to become stronger. And each time finding or redefining our purpose gives life meaning, which gives us hope. Finding the hope hidden in our hearts is how we heal. It is not just our imperative. It is our responsibility in our own healing process.

And so, while loss will come and go in our lives, there is life at the end of grief. It is our choice to embrace loss and move forward as we once again become the masters of our future.

It
wasn't
supposed
to end
this way

Astoundingly High White Count
June 2010

Jeanette, my love,

I must tell you this period of absence has made me acutely aware of all that you mean to me. I knew I loved you dearly, but I had no idea how profoundly you effect me, my desires, my wishes for a life together. You are the centerpiece of my life.

Robert Canady, written May 16, 1995

In hopes Dr. Abrahm would see me, I poke my head out from behind the curtains separating the cubicles.

"Jeanette, what are you doing in the emergency room? Is your mother okay?"

My mother is one of Dr. Abrahm's patients. It does not surprise me he immediately assumes she is the one who is ill. At eighty-four, while her little, bent-over body is frail, she repeatedly ignores all physician predictions she will not last much longer. It is as if she has become immune to dire prognostications.

But we are not in the emergency room for Mom. Not tonight.

"Mom's fine, Dr. Abrahm. It's Bob."

He frowns as though finding pieces of a puzzle that do not fit.

"Bob?" His slightly grey eyebrows arch. "What's wrong?"

"Abdominal pain." I speak quickly, knowing he has been called to the ER for the patient in the cubicle next to us. I am stealing his time from her. But the gut is Dr. Abrahm's specialty, and he is the doctor's doctor in this well-heeled community, and he is the one I want to see Bob, and he is the one who stood by me when my first husband fell ill, and he is the one who touches my arm when he notices I'm scared.

"I'll be there in a minute, Jeanette."

The air I have been holding in my lungs releases.

We chat, Bob and I. We chat about the hospital, the attentive nurses, the IV tube, the curtains, anything because we know nothing yet. Chatter puts a blanket over things unknown.

Dr. Abrahm walks in with a quizzical expression.

"Bob, you have an astoundingly high white count." I can see the concern on the doctor's face. He is referring to the number of white blood cells in my husband's blood, the very cells that protect his body from infection. Dr. Abrahm knows I understand a lot of medical terminology. He has known me through almost thirty years of my own illnesses, my first husband's illness, and my mother's complicated health issues. I do not know if he realizes Bob has no clue, no hint as to the meaning of the words, "astoundingly high white count."

At times, Dr. Abrahm's words have a way of piercing into my brain. His words are always short, pointed, but backed with caring the size of an elephant. *Astoundingly high white count.* I scan my mind for medical information about high white counts, but Bob has no temperature, and he has no obvious signs of infection. *What the hell is going on here?* My thoughts flash from one possible cause to another, eliminating each faster than the last until it slows and focuses on one: leukemia. I place my hands on the simple, plastic chair and sit down carefully, quietly, saying nothing. I reach for my husband's hand, just to feel his skin, to experience the strength of his gentle grip, but my abdominal muscles tighten like a fighter waiting for the next blow.

Surely, there would have been clues. What am I missing?

The naps. All those naps Bob has taken for some time now. He cherished those naps as a benefit of retirement, of not having to keep schedules, a gentle rebuffing of all the organizations he used to run that demanded his time for so many years. *The low platelet count.* The steady but thimble-sized change in his platelet count was not low enough to concern his physicians, but a trend I had noticed while reading Bob's lab reports. I have learned to review lab reports as I follow my own numerous medical conditions, as well as Mother's complicated case. I always spot any results outside the normal range. With a mind in over-drive, I wonder now if platelets drop with leukemia. I can't quite make sense of all the pieces, and that plagues me. After several years of working in a university medical center, I know too much, but not enough.

Done with his consult, Doctor Abrahm exits the emergency room leaving the ER hospitalist on staff to manage Bob's case. It is a new system, the use of hospitalists, but it allows the private physicians to avoid the haphazard life of being on-call. This new hospitalist seems too young to have graduated from medical school, let alone completed an internship and a residency. Her eyes are a rich, deep brown; her expression is calm. Her long, straight, black hair falls down her small, petite back. I quietly hope with her youth comes the most recent information from medical school.

Bob's eyes focus on her as she stands on the other side of the gurney, directly across from me. I know the expression he wears on his face, the one when his smile stalls and his dimples stop dancing, the one that shows his concentration, his instincts for obtaining facts. I see no fear. Bob has no idea what Dr. Abrahm's words can imply, but Bob would not show fear. Not here, not now.

She says, "Mr. Canady, you have a very high white blood cell count. That can suggest several possibilities."

I stand by the bed in the tiny cubicle wondering if our world will change in an instant.

"Your body could be reacting to some kind of hidden infection, but you have no temperature or any obvious signs of infection that we can find. Or you could have developed a leukemic reaction. Since we are not sure why your white count is high, or why you are having abdominal pain, it would be best if we admitted you and completed some additional tests."

I place my hand on the bed's guardrail to steady myself. I have to ask. It may be hard for both of us to hear, but *I have to ask.* "Doctor, are you looking for leukemia?"

Bob quickly turns his face toward me. His eyes widen with surprise, and his face turns back to the physician.

She lowers her head in the slightest way, as if avoiding looking directly at either of us, but recovers gracefully and places her gaze on Bob. "Yes, we are. We need to confirm it or rule it out. We'll call in an oncology consult to review your case." It seems so odd that she stands there—three feet from me—talking about my husband and leukemia, and my mind is so stunned I can't figure out how to pronounce her name.

As she leaves, it seems the noise in the emergency room fades into the distance, as though Bob and I are drifting alone on some isolated island in the middle of nowhere. My frustration that my husband did not wake me last night while in so much pain melts into concern. I want to climb over these steel guardrails that keep him in the bed and me at a distance. I want to hold him. He reaches for my hand.

Now, lying on the emergency room gurney, this six-foot, two hundred pound, muscle-laden man who, at 80, can still pick me up and set me on our bed at will, seems to need my protection. But I can't. I don't know how to protect him from his own white blood cells.

Bob draws in a deep breath. "Well, I guess I'll be staying in here for a couple of days. Why don't you head home?"

It's past midnight, my husband is facing the prospects of leukemia, and he is worried about me. "I'm not leaving until you are upstairs, and in your hospital room." I can't. I don't know how to walk out of the emergency room. I don't know how to leave him there alone.

A lab tech appears, and pulls the curtain back a few inches. She carries her compact, white basket organized by sections of needles, tape, alcohol wipes and stretchable plastic bands that trap blood at just the right spot so it can be drawn, and that is what she does to Bob's arm.

The nurse, whom I am convinced, has angel wings hidden under her uniform, stops by to tell us Bob will be transferred to the 8th floor. My heart sinks. The eighth floor is the best floor, with the best nurses in the hospital. It is also the cancer floor, but Bob does not know that. I wish I did not. I stroke Bob's arm lightly, so my touch gives no indication I am stuck, petrified from numbness.

A staffer shows up ready to transport Bob upstairs. I know the halls of this hospital well. My mother has been here many times. My first husband was here before he died. I have studied the pictures of major donors and board members gracing the walls, yet tonight all the corridors look the same, all the pictures blend together. All my eyes can see is Bob on a gurney. All my mind can hear is the word, "leukemia." It seems so odd he may have cancer in his blood, yet I swear I can feel it in mine.

"Jeanette, it's getting so late. I really think you should go. You still have a drive ahead of you."

Bob is in his room, a private room, like all patients have on this floor. The risk of infection to immune systems that have been pummeled by cancer and different types of toxic chemos earns these patients the right to privacy. I watch the team take over Bob's care. They examine his body for skin tears, complete the medical history, and even explain when he can expect blood draws. They amaze me. I hate this floor.

"Well, you are checked in and in good hands. You need to sleep, and you're right, I do have a drive ahead of me." I lean over and kiss him, and then walk toward the door. I turn, walk back to the bed and kiss him again. Then I kiss him again. I don't want to walk out the door. I want to stay here, on the eighth floor, the floor I hate that has the man I love.

We are looking for leukemia. The phrase rattles around in my mind the whole drive home, ricocheting from one corner of my brain to another as though if I let these words sink in, they will take on a life of their own. But I make it home, drive onto the driveway, open the garage door, and pull my aging car into the unkempt garage.

And then it hits. He is not at home. He is not with me in the car, and I start to cry. I cry so hard I cannot see the dashboard. I cry so hard I am sure my heart is cracking, maybe my vocal cords ripping. I cry because I somehow know what is coming, and I would give anything to not go down this path. But if he does, I must.

I pull myself together and walk into the house.

Brace yourself, Jeanette. He needs you.

A Stolen Kiss
September 1994

The fire between us started seventeen years ago. Our initial
meetings were sparse, and born of professional academic
interests. Then one day, he startled me as he leaned
forward in an elevator and kissed me quickly on the lips.
Holding my notebook against my chest, sounding like a
mother scolding a child, my words marched from my mouth,
"Bob Canady, you stop that!" The next day he came looking
for me, eyes cast downward, embarrassed by his own lapse
of judgment.

"Jeanette, I have to apologize for my behavior
yesterday. It wasn't like me. I've become so fond of you, I'm
not sure I can continue our friendship. It's just getting too
difficult for me."

One only needed to be in this man's presence to
feel his integrity. I fully expected he would search for me,
embarrassed by his actions. I listened with my heart and
spoke my truth.

"I understand and I will accept whatever decision
you make. I really hope our friendship can continue. It
means a great deal to me."

But I knew he felt the little snaps of electricity that
bounced from one of us to the other. After our quarterly
lunches, I would chastise myself for having laughed too
easily, for being so wrapped up in his words. The difference
between us was a simple one: he acknowledged the shocks
of energy; I tried desperately to deny them.

It was not his physique, the color of his eyes, nor the
style of his clothes that caught my attention at our first
meeting. I might not have been able to describe him had I
been asked to the following day. I only noticed he seemed a

7

bit clumsy, a bit overweight. It took time for me to notice he had a nice smile and crystal blue eyes that, upon closer examination, danced in tandem with his wit.

He used that wit to make me laugh, and with time it sent my insides quivering like invisible foreplay, transparent hands running over my body. I do not remember specific words or phrases he used, yet when I recall those infrequent lunches, my body can still feel the sensations shimmy down my neck and into my back.

He was a master at controlling behavior, and he knew how to flirt to the edge of safety, an edge that did not test my ability to hold my ground. The elevator kiss was an aberration, a misstep, but it was his misstep.

My need to be held and comforted must have been obvious to Bob, as I am sure it was to many, but I had to keep my balance. I was married to Jack, and while he was not a faithful man, Jack was dying. Temptations had come and gone through the years, so I erected boundaries around my body more than my heart. To me, fidelity was no longer a commitment to my mate, but represented my decision to live comfortably within my conscience. The line in the sand I would not cross was my own. It was only fair Bob know I was married—to a dying man.

It was a life of parallel tracks as though two trains chugged along side-by-side. I was losing my first husband on one set of rails, and fighting my feelings for another man on a second set. I had no reason for guilt. Caring for Jack was more immediate, more important. Bob, once he understood the challenge before me, was careful to not tip this delicate boat, so he supported me from a distance, a safety zone for both of us.

Eventually, Bob offered to help me with one of my consulting projects. He would call once a week to discuss the client, yet always started with, "How's Jack? How are you holding up?" He set his feelings aside to shore mine up. I doubt either of us realized he was unpeeling my resistance one layer at a time. In retrospect, he was. Still, I busied myself with setting boundaries and keeping my focus on my husband who edged closer and closer to death until on Christmas Day 1994, Jack died.

I doubt I told Bob how much his kindness touched my heart as Jack failed over time. I do not know if I could have expressed it with clarity, but the kindnesses he extended when my emotional pain shot higher than a rocket helped me find my balance at a time when life seemed to have no balance at all.

* * *

It was at Jack's Celebration of Life I became acutely aware of my affection for Bob. He was amused. I nearly fainted, and it was all Sherri's fault. A long time best friend, she approached Bob as he prepared to leave the event.

"Oh, you must be Bob Canady. Jeanette has told me *so much* about you." Her emphasis on "so much" stopped the conversation somewhat faster than a lightning bolt. He glanced at me briefly, tilted his head, then focused his blue-eyed gaze on Sherri.

"Oh? And what have you heard?" My inhalation was short, but fast, as I tried to recall what I had said about him. Had I mentioned more than his kindness? His intelligence?

I still have no memory of her answer, but cannot forget the give-away grin on her face, or the curious expression on his. Their conversation continued as though I had left the room. I stepped back, leaned against a railing and attempted to catch the breath lost in my lungs causing my head to feel light. He was the dean of one of the largest business schools in Southern California. I was a graduate student. *What the hell was she doing?*

Yet, instinctively I knew. Her eyes peered through my heart, and she heard the deeper meaning in my words, meanings I shoved aside as I wrapped myself in a bubble. She was going to direct a small breeze on this quiet fire; she was going to watch to see if the embers lit. They talked for some time, then he walked out the door, out the front gate, got into his classic Mercedes and drove away.

* * *

Months passed while I grieved the loss of my husband. I dropped out of the academic program, put my home up for sale, and watched my business tank as I meandered through the fog of grief.

One day, Bob called to see how I was doing. I suspect I told him the sad condition of my consulting business. He explained he had a consulting partner, a graduate of a masters program at the university. They had a client in need of coaching, and he asked if I would like to work with them. It was a generous offer. His voice gave no hint of pity, or rescue, or even an excuse to see me. He simply wanted to help. Helping others was automatic for Bob, as though imbedded in his genetic code. Another layer of my resistance began to peel back.

"Why don't we meet and talk about the project?"

I consented.

We met on a Sunday morning. He arrived first and waved when I walked in the door. Even in a business meeting, the warmth of his smile was unmistakable. Yet, since that day in the elevator, his behavior failed to cross questionable boundaries as he focused on the project, what my role would be, and how we might work together. Then he mentioned he was planning to relocate to Georgia.

"Georgia? How would we work together with you in Georgia?"

"We would meet at the client's place of business. Just fly in." His logical response seemed lost in the sudden onset of emotions that began to churn inside me.

Excusing myself, I walked down the hall to the bathroom, stepped inside and closed the door. *He's moving? He can't move.* But of course he could. It was his life, his prerogative. *How the hell am I going keep my emotions in check working with him?*

We talked for a while after I returned to the table, then walked outside. The asphalt was covered with cars, lined up neatly side-by-side in the cramped parking lot. We sat in his Mercedes, both of us reluctant to end the conversation. It was time for me to come clean.

"Bob, if we are going to work together, I think we should discuss our relationship."

"What about it?"

I chose my words carefully, still reeling over the death of my husband while fighting emotions that kept seeping into my soul each time I talked with this man.

"Well, you have been a wonderful friend, and I love you dearly for that." I held my thumb and my finger up, measuring about an inch between them. "But I am this close to falling in love with you, and I do not need to do that." I paused momentarily, about to explain how important it was for me to maintain my perspective when his words broke through my thoughts.

"I'm in love with you." His tone was factual and calm, as though giving me the score of a basketball game.

I stuttered, continued to look forward out the windshield, and sat there chatting, words tumbling out of my mouth, certainly in some kind of order, but clearly lacking in relevance. Then he leaned over, turned my face toward him, and kissed me. This was not an elevator peck, but a warm, tender kiss that intensified the passions stirring inside my body. This kiss was not stolen.

My thought was singular. *Oh my God, I'm in trouble. This man can even kiss.*

It was a simple act—that kiss—but pivotal. He walked me to my car, opened my door, wrapped his strong arms around me filling me with a sense of giddiness and fear. Then, as he held me close, he reached far down my back with his strong, but gentle hands, and patted my behind.

Oh God, I'm his. He owns me now.

The courses of our two lives were forever changed.

* * *

At first, I tried to pull back, to find my footing, so I kept the distance of time between us. Two weeks later he came to my house. The bounce in his step was too easy, too ready for my state of mind, which was still grieving, still frightened by the power of my feelings for this new man. I held on to what little resistance I had left. Skilled at reading people, he stood at the far end of the kitchen, leaned against the counter and smiled.

My arms folded, my posture erect, my words peppered the air. "What is it you want from me?"

His expression changed as his eyebrows rose and his eyes focused directly on me. "What do you think I want?"

"I, uh, well, um, I don't mean to be bold, but I think you want me."

"Right."

"And I think you want me for life."

"Right again." His reply was so simple, so direct, so uncomplicated, there was only one response I could muster.

"Oh."

It was as if someone had taken every emotion known to man, poured them into a large vat and began to stir.

"So you are not going to move?"

"No, I'm not going to move, Jeanette."

Flattered and frightened, I kissed him goodbye and sent him home.

It was my mother who listened to my elation, my fear, my confusion. "He's such a wonderful man, Mom. He's kind and caring. He's smart. He's really smart. And he says he's in love with me." She listened at the other end of the line, always patient, always supportive.

"Mom, I don't know what to do."

"I know what I'd do."

"Really? What?"

"Jeanette, I'd trip him and beat him to the floor."

It was sound advice coming from a 68-year-old mother, but I kept it to myself. Her advice required contemplation, honest examination, but more than anything, her advice required a plan. And so, I planned.

Two weeks later I invited Bob to visit again. I hesitated briefly when he knocked on the front door. My steps were slow, even deliberate. A blanket lay on the living room floor, warmed by the wispy flames in the fireplace. I opened the door in silky attire designed to be removed, slowly, erotically.

He must have known this was coming. He must have. He brought a bottle of champagne.

Transitions
May 1995

What a day! I spent every effort to reach you today with absolutely no success. How this troubled me. I was so saddened and frustrated. How I miss you. How empty I feel. As I neared my mailbox, all that changed. I saw your letter from London on your way to Nairobi. I was so excited I could hardly open the box. I read your letter twice and will read it again before going to sleep tonight. I love you so very much.
Robert Canady, May 11, 1995

It was sixteen years ago, almost to the day I boarded a plane and flew to Africa.

It was my realtor's idea. After Jack died, Laraine sat at my kitchen table and listed my house. I began to cry.

"Everything is gone, Laraine. My husband died, my business tanked while caring for my husband, and now I have to sell my home. Everything is gone."

She looked at me. "Jeanette, there are two ways to look at this. You can say the glass is half empty or you can say, 'I have a new slate on which to write the rest of my life.'"

I blotted the tears in my eyes, and looked at Laraine as I tried to reframe my thoughts. In the midst of grief, it was difficult to even consider embracing a new life. Yet, the subtle message was profound: a half empty glass is passive; a clean slate, pen in hand, is to control one's destiny.

"So," she said, "what have you always wanted to do in life?"

There was no hesitation from me. "Go to Africa."

Laraine stood up, walked to my phone, dialed the operator, and obtained the number for British Airways. She spoke briefly to customer service, then turned and said, "Eighteen hundred dollars. When do you want to book the flight?"

I had to run. While my new love, Bob, gave me such comfort, I still felt the loss of my first husband. So I had to run far enough to process a life passed, and give way to a new life. It was a tough month for Bob, but it was a healing month for me. The love he and I shared was so fresh ripples of warm currents flowed from his finger tips to mine at the slightest touch of our hands. New love has such mystical powers. But it was also authentic, as the sense of melting into each other's souls felt so warm, so very safe.

* * *

I landed in Nairobi at night, and could feel Africa much the way I had sensed her since childhood as though this incredible continent was part of my emotional past. The acacia trees, silhouetted against the night sky, branches quietly reaching to the sides, so reminiscent of the land's elegant mystery. I turned off the music in my room to hear the crickets, frogs and even birds outside my window. As the hands of my watch approached midnight, nature's rhythms seemed to come and go at will.

I sat at the small desk in my room to write to Bob.

How much precious time have I wasted not making my current moment my heaven? My life has been difficult,

*and I color my time, my experiences
with painful, lonely colors, but you
bring such depth and intimacy to my
life.*

    *Thank you for helping me see
what I have with you. You never gave up
on me—now, don't ever let me go.*

I sent my letters home to him. He could not send the letters he wrote, knowing our tour moved from one park to another sometimes within a day, so he kept them for me knowing that, upon my return, we would read our words together so the flow of our letters could match the tempo of our hearts.

Later, one of his letters read:

    *Well, my Love, it is near midnight
and today was wonderful, exhilarating
and sad! Sad because, again, I could
not reach you by phone nor fax. My how
I tried! I miss you terribly. I saved your
last phone message as you arrived in
Nairobi. I listen to it frequently ... I love
to hear your voice as it brings you near
to me.*

    *It is so hard for me to realize the
impact of your being away. It's terrible.
I feel so lonely it seems I will never be
able to hold you and tell you how much
I love you!*

At times, I shared his ache during the day. Mostly, I marveled at the steps I had taken toward a lifelong relationship with him. It seemed inconceivable I could be falling in love with one man while mourning the loss of another, but like joy does not consume sadness, sadness does not consume joy. They co-exist in life. The same day I wrote to him.

Robert,

I have never written a love letter. As I sit in the heart of Kenya, contemplating Isaac Dinesen and her lover, now seems to be the time. The connection they shared was more than love - they communicated without words and glances - they shared thoughts deep within their minds and by what means, who knows? How else would she have known of his death before hearing the news?

We want the same, you and I. To know someone so intimately has always been my dream. So complete is your knowledge of me, I am naked with you. At times, you know my thoughts before I know them myself.

It seems our spirits dance together, ebbing and flowing with the music we create. The fighter becomes the *ballet master, and the ballerina succumbs to the dance. The only need is to be in rhythm.*

What you give to me in this dance is profound. How is it we know each other so well? Have we danced to this music at a different place? Have our souls met at another time? The oneness of our spirits has qualities of the divine, so pure, so sweet. The light you bring into my life is one only a soul mate could bring.

When you touch me, my senses cannot help but respond. The feel of your chest against mine, the sensuality of your kiss, the firm, gentle touch of your hands reach the core of my emotions ever beckoning me closer. My tears reveal the intense response you create in me when we make love. My need to love you merges with my need to be one with you.

Robert, my sweet, I adore you. Promise me this—that you will never stop adoring me.

All my love from Kenya, J

Yet in the midst of love, I needed distance. Tears of grief came and went at will, whether driving down a dirt road searching for elephants, or giraffes, or a pride of lions. Africa's pull was strong, even seductive as I watched thousands of wildebeest, noses sniffing the air, hooves pounding the ground sounding like a great train as they ran toward the rain.

All things have mystery in Africa, not unlike the love in my heart and the grief in my soul.

It must have been the spirit of Tanzania's Lake Manyara that allowed me to move more fully from one life to another, to a time when thoughts of loss were fewer and thoughts of love more frequent.

The dirt road to Lake Manyara Lodge curled up a mountain side, flush with thick, deep green foliage. The Lake Manyara National Park, directly below, spread over 125 square miles and teemed with animal and plant species of all kinds. Even at 3,100 feet above sea level, this park covered five vegetation zones. At the bottom of the mountain, the groundwater fed a green forest so thick monkeys and baboons controlled the under bush and swung in the trees. The elephants, tall and as broad as tanks, were the power in the acacia woodlands. The impalas, necks long and graceful, and legs built for speed when facing a predator, stayed close to the elephants as they grazed the land for its abundant foliage. The acacia trees were of such strength the lions were known to climb the branches to recline as formally anointed kings. The other animals did not challenge their position.

In the sunlight, Lake Manyara appeared to be a sliver of a lake from the lodge high on the hillside. And she was a sliver – all 35 miles of her length were slender and shallow. She glistened with a sedate shimmer of bouncing light, but she was never more than five feet deep at any point, as if nature put a pond right in that spot to entice the animals to play without fear. The terrain hugging the edges of the lake seemed almost barren in contrast to the rest of the land in the park. When the season was right, thousands of flamingos appeared as if a solid pink work of art floated on the shallow water.

Our Maasai guide, Victor, gave me permission to walk outside the compound at the lodge. Down the road, the local Tanzanian community was well above the park as was the lodge. I wanted to explore.

"Fifteen minutes out and back," he told me. "And don't talk to anyone!"

I was sure Victor had a reason, but how does one not talk to the children who were so excited to find a person from another land walking in their community? *Jambo, jambo!* they yelled, "hello" in Swahili. Two little ones ran to show me their catch—a beautiful chameleon—hoping I could buy it, or at least trade a pen for it. The adults waved and smiled as they herded their goats back into their community for the evening, while one of their "goatlets" bounced over to me to play.

Grief washes away in such peace.

As the sun began to sink into the horizon, I started my journey back, thoughts full of my new love. Suddenly, I heard a deep growl, yet not a growl I could identify. A donkey brayed and ran through underbrush so dense, the donkey was never visible. The growling animal was large enough to make a donkey run, and there I stood, on the edge of a forest so thick, the predator that could not be seen could have no name.

I froze on the road, listening intently. The donkey was quiet. The predator was quiet. The silence was a good sign, indicating a stalemate or a failed attack. But the silence failed to make me feel comfortable knowing I must come closer to the forest to return to the lodge, knowing I must pass by the dense brush where a predator may be waiting, and wishing I had Bob's muscle-bound strength beside me. I had no weapon, cell phones were useless here, nor had I brought one on the trip. Even my watch was worthless, as nothing could keep the sun from setting into darkness. The villagers were in their huts now, pets and children protected by the community. Within minutes, a truck appeared. I flagged these men down, men unknown to me, in an unknown land, and climbed into their truck. Our languages did not cross barriers, but they knew where I belonged and returned me to the lodge. *Asante,* I told them in Swahili as they drove away, knowing the predator, whatever it was, would not have me for dinner.

That night, I lay in bed, restless and queasy from some new food in my stomach. It was a challenging time to become nauseous, as the generators and the water had been shut down for the night. In the quiet of my discomfort, I wondered what else I might have done differently in my relationship with Jack. He became so angry when he was dying. Could I have disarmed his anger rather than confronting him? Was I supposed to have learned forgiveness? Perhaps it is through loss that we learn how to forgive.

I imagined how happy Jack would have been to be alive, to be with me in this remarkable land with her animals and her people. I thanked him for making this last trip possible. I thanked him for the good times, the times when we were able to love completely. I thanked him for trying when trying was difficult for him.

At midnight, I peered out the glass doors over the valley and across the lake. I watched immense clouds move in and hover over the lake absorbing the moon's light, then defusing it across the span of the water. The water began to glow as though made of silver. It seemed as if the heavens were speaking to me.

My new love danced in my mind. I pulled him to me, imagining his arms around me, feeling his kiss. I pulled hard as though I could send him some sense of this amazing sight, this picture I carried in my mind. Holding on to someone half way around the world is much like holding on to someone who is gone from this plane. A soul can feel a presence even when the eyes cannot see.

On the other side of the world, Bob wrote to me:

My love and desire to be with you is so deep, resulting in my heartache (literally) for you. I feel I would rather die than lose you or not be with you— thought I would never say that ...ever!

In all this, I hope you find peace. I will accept you deserve the best in love, support, and the opportunity to grow in any dimension your heart desires.

Just remember - I am here for you. I long for a loving, blissful, spiritual life together.

All my love forever,
Robert

I climbed out of my bed, opened the glass doors, and stepped onto my balcony, feeling the night. The moon shared her energy, and for that moment, Lake Manyara and her beauty existed only for me. I began to release the memory of one love and embrace the future with another.

Two weeks later I returned to California. I landed at LAX, dashed through customs, and started for baggage claim. As I walked down the long corridor and turned a corner, there stood a man named Robert among the throngs of people and drivers waiting for tired travelers from Africa. He held a small sign, with large black letters carefully printed in two simple words:

JEANETTE REESE

I was home. At last.

Roots of Honor
1940s

His childhood was simple. Bob grew up on a farm in the Deep South of Georgia during the 1930s, with his parents and two sisters. I was charmed by the stories as I sat and listened to Bob, his sisters and their husbands retell the old tales of earlier days gone by. To a California gal born in the 1950's, whose history did not touch the Great Depression or the impact of World War II, the Southern stories were like gold from a world far away. At Bob's class reunions, I videotaped his classmates, capturing this place and time the best I could. When I had videotaped all surviving class members, I interviewed them in groups and wrote stories the local paper was kind enough to publish. This is what I heard…

The town was named Screven—more village than town—with acres of plowed land, rivers and streams meandering through the countryside of pines and cedars soaking up the land's moisture. The trees were draped with vines that gave coverage to an occasional swamp alligator. Farm pigs that escaped their owners grew tusks like wild pigs within months of freedom, adding mystery to the dense foliage. At times, a bootlegger would hide his still amidst these trees and bushes that rose from the swampy land. When the pigs happened on to the alcohol-loaded mulch discarded by a bootlegger, they ate voraciously, squealing and grunting with delight, tipping off the local sheriff as to the location of the still.

As Bob told it, there would be no stills in his family. They were Hard Shell Baptists who sat in church listening to the preacher speak of sin and God for most of the day each Sunday. While the church used much of a farming family's day off, it connected each person to a morality that bound the community like a warm blanket through difficult times and hard harvest seasons. Love Thy Neighbor might not have been perfectly put into practice as a value, but if a family fell on hard times, the community would come together, bringing casseroles, helping with farm equipment, often sharing one of the few cars in the village.

Even today in Screven, children are bred by two parents but parented by many, including neighbors, preachers, teachers, and principals. Bob learned about such social control at an early age when he misled his father. At ten years old, Bob had already started his third business. He would "pull up the peanuts" on the family farm, boil them in an old black iron pot, bag them, then carry the peanuts two miles to town to sell them. He would stand in front of the local grocery until each five cent bag was sold, then follow his ten-year-old nose as it traced the aroma of Mrs. Meadow's hot dog stand.

One day, he walked by the drug store, and noticed a slot machine in grand display near the front door. It occurred to him he could turn that $2.00 peanut bag profit into some serious revenue, so he took his earnings, coin by coin, dropped them into the slot, and pulled that handle until his worn pockets were empty.

His father inquired about the money. Bob said he had lost it. Unbeknownst to Bob, his father had already heard about the loss from a neighbor who had seen the young boy pulling the arm on the mechanical bandit, so he gave his son one more chance to speak the whole truth— which Bob failed to do.

Bob told me he got a whuppin' that day, a tough one with a young branch from the peach tree in the backyard, a whuppin' that was tough to bear, as his favorite grandmother was visiting and saw that switch hit the back of his trousers. Not telling the truth was, according to Bob, lying so he believed his father taught him a great moral lesson. It was a hard way to learn about humiliation and truth, but he learned. Throughout his life, he fine-tuned that morality until it was finally cemented in his bones.

As a child of the Great Depression, few of his friends' families had wealth beyond the spiritual realm. As one of his classmates told it with a hint of a smile, "None of us knew we was poor, because we all done lived the same." There were no luxurious items, no expensive homes or cars, but his Grandpa owned a truck. It was for farm use, but that truck took family to church on Sundays, and sometimes to town for groceries. His parents used their mule and wagon for transportation, the same mule that would let the kids climb up on her back as they played. Once she tired of it, she would bend her neck toward the ground and cause those rascals to slip down her neck like a slide. Entertainment was cheap.

The family lived on what was called a two-horse farm. It took two horses to plant and till the amount of land they owned, but they owned one, along with that trusty mule, a couple of milk cows, a few hogs for meat, and some goats. His parents had purchased the farm, with its small shack of a home, from Grandpa Miller, and they grew corn and cotton, tobacco and tomatoes, and sometimes slipped in some soybeans, always rotating crops to keep the soil rich with nutrients.

Soon after his parents moved to the farm, Bob's father cut down some trees on his new land, hauled the lumber to a local mill and walked out with enough wood to build a "tenant house." It was small, but had a kitchen, living room, fireplace, two bedrooms, and one porch, as Bob described it. A two-horse farm was too big, required too much labor for his father, so a share cropper family moved in to help with the workload. At one time, a black couple with two children occupied the tenant house. Bob's parents taught him and his sisters to be respectful, so they called the parents by titles: Aunt Rhodie and Uncle Will. Direct use of a first name would have caused a scolding by his elders.

When I saw the farm almost seventy years later, his parents' old home lay humbled like a pile of bones under the limbs of an old tree that had grown untrimmed and unchecked over the yard. But even when Bob was a small tyke, his parent's wooden house was old, its roof made of tin. It still stood proud, almost as proud as his parents were to have their own farm. There was no electricity, but they owned an ice box to keep their food cold with the help of the ice man who came twice a week. The outhouse, as Bob described it, was about 100 yards from the house. The cold must have chilled those little buns as they headed for that singular shed in the wintertime.

In Screven, like so many communities, porches functioned like a local pub where people sat, discussed God and politics, but mostly told stories. They may not have had a need for alcohol, but the stories would flow like a river. Neighbors and friends didn't always agree, as Bob remembered, especially when the topic of bird dogs came up. Bob's Grandpa used to say, "I never seen a feller who didn't think his own bird dawg weren't the best to be had." This old house on his parent's new farm had a porch, a porch with two tempting rocking chairs just waiting for someone to spin a tale.

It was a neighbor, not a life guard at a community pool as one might find today, but the grandfather of one of Bob's friends who taught the kids how to swim. Mr. Davis, as Bob told the story, was a slender man in his late sixties, an expert fiddler and banjo player. Music floated from the Davis farm across the quiet fields and through the whispering pines, as most of the Davis folks played the guitar, banjo, fiddle or mandolin. When Mr. Davis wasn't pickin' his banjo, he was hauling five or ten kids in his mule-drawn cart, heading through the woods and the swamp down to the river. He would unload the kids, hitch his mule to the tree, and don his 1920's swimsuit. Bob said his parents did not want him near the water until he could swim. Mr. Davis believed in swimming by "baptism," so he would grab a kid by the feet and flip him backwards into the slow moving river, laughing the whole time. His patience was impenetrable. Hard to tell how many kids learned to swim with Mr. Davis, but not a one drowned.

Most Christmases were lean, matched by the leanness of a country in hard times, and the yield of crops in the field. Toys were rare in Bob's life. The only real toy he described to me was a small tricycle his parents bought him for Christmas one year. He rode his "kiddy car" until he broke the pedal off, which sank his little heart. The toys under the Christmas trees of today would have seemed like walking into the home of a Rockefeller to Bob and his sisters. To them, a toy or two was a luxury, but so was the gift of the coconut in the shell, or the orange, or the cluster of grapes that completed the gift package. Any present seemed to give Bob a sense of wealth as he had no other point of reference, nor did he care. He was happy.

But he was not so enthusiastic about school. Kindergarten was not available in the tiny Screven School System. There were 25 students in his first grade class, and they traveled through each grade together. They bonded like brothers and sisters, but that was not how it started for Bob. After he arrived for his first day of first grade, the blonde-haired, blue-eyed kid with dimples that danced, decided against school, decided he did not like it, so he slipped outside and walked two and a half miles home. The next day he did the same thing. The third day, his mother sent his younger sister with him. She stayed, they played, and the next day he went to school on his own. It was a rocky start for a man who joined the military to get an education, and ended up with two masters degrees and a doctorate.

If Bob wanted anything, he found a way to work for it. When he was about six years old, his Uncle Ray gave him a small goat to raise. Living on a farm, he understood animals bred to create offspring, and soon he had located a mate for his goat. Eventually, he bought a breeder, and before long he had a small herd with one mean Billy Goat that would put his head down and chase both Bob's sisters right out of the fields. To this day, his sisters remember that goat. I suspect his parents were not thrilled their daughters, barely past toddler years, were the target of some nasty goat with sharp horns.

Bob finally found, "an unusual market for my grown goats," a profitable way to unload his herd, so he sold them to townspeople hosting community "goat roasts" to raise money for local politicians. Once his young entrepreneurial mind began to whirr, it was not easily stopped. He had one goal in mind: he wanted a bicycle he could ride into town. Then, that doggone Billy Goat attacked his baby sister, causing him to close out his little business altogether—but not before he bought his new bike.

He once wrote that he picked cotton in the fields, sometimes alongside the black sharecroppers who sang and chanted in harmony, maintaining the pace of the picking, in a dialect not easily understood by other workers. At the end of the day, he would watch as these hard-working folks stood around the scales awaiting the "call out" of how much cotton had been picked. A good day meant more money, and a celebration of laughter and jokes would ripple through the pickers.

The new farm added to everyone's responsibilities. His mother worked alongside her husband in the fields, and tended the house. It was hard work planting, growing, and harvesting crops and every hand was needed, including the small ones. Bob's father's passion was that farm, and he wanted his son to stay home from school to help till the land.

His mother had different ideas. Her children would have an education, but before school started, and as soon as it was out for the day, they had their chores. Bob learned to love education, in part because his brain was a fine one, but also because he learned to dislike tending anything green that sprouted from the soil.

At one of his class reunions, a classmate told me, "I wanted to try picking cotton. One day, I did it all day long. I made one dollar! I decided right then and there if I had to pick cotton, I'd rather starve."

Another of his friends shared, "As soon as we got home, we changed into our work clothes and worked the fields 'til sundown. Then we still had to study."

He was days shy of his thirteenth birthday when his father's heart, the third generation of hearts that did not pump well, failed. Bob was by his side as his father looked up at his own father-in-law and asked him to watch over his family. And Grandpa Miller did. Bob, his mother, and two sisters moved from the farm they were buying to a small tenant house on Grandpa Miller's farm. It was similar to the house they had lost, a simple wooden structure, no electricity, no running water, and no bathroom. But there was a pump on the back porch, and an outhouse in the backyard. Bob studied and read by the light from a lantern.

The wood shutters kept out some of the cold, but the fires in the kitchen and the living room kept the house bearable.

With no farm of their own, mother and children searched for additional income to survive. The family picked tobacco, too. Bob would earn a couple of dollars a day, but as he told it, with fruits and vegetables from his Grandpa's farm, the week's grocery bill rarely passed a three dollar mark.

He was born a leader. By the time he was sixteen, he was put in charge of a tobacco warehouse, a large barn with an office and a bathroom. Women were not allowed to work the warehouse, but he had some twenty workers under him, each one a prisoner of war from Nazi Germany. The POWs most likely came from nearby Fort Stewart, but some installation camps had satellite camps of 250 to 750 men across parts of Georgia. They supplied much needed workers for local farmers in a draft-drained labor pool. It was tough work, and when the prisoners worked hard, Bob would buy them a Coca Cola as a reward. One day when a local man mistook Bob for another teen who had done him wrong, the POWs stepped in to protect their youthful leader. Years later, when Bob happened onto one of them in another state, by then a freed man who had worked off his debt against America and had chosen to stay, the German still remembered his kindness.

At the class reunions, I learned Bob was also a born prankster, at least when he was around his best friend, Elwood. Mr. Zalumas is a name remembered by many a Screven kid for he was the high school principal. He might never have taken the job had he met Bob and Elwood before he accepted the position. Until the day they died, those two friends broke up in stitches and knee-slappin' guffaws telling the story of Mr. Zalumas' Lincoln Zephyr. As Elwood told me, "We picked up the front end of that car and hitched it over a post 'bout 18 inches high. We were watchin' from the window when Mr. Zalumas went to get in his car. He looked at the car, scratched his head, and headed over to our classroom. He says, 'Elwood, you two fellers wanna come out here, and help me with my car?'" Elwood paused at this point of the story, building the suspense, shifting in his chair, trying to stifle that grin just a bit longer. Bob would play along, but his eyes would twinkle—a dead give-a-way a good punch line was about to be delivered.

"Yep," Elwood continued to tell me, "I told him, 'Sure Mr. Zalumas.' When the three of us walked up to the car, I stood right there and said, 'Well now, look at that! Wonder who did that to your car?'"

Bob liked to tell the story about how he and Elwood set a smoke bomb under the hood of the same Lincoln Zephyr. They rigged it so once the engine started, the smoke poured out from under the hood. Hard to tell where those two found a smoke bomb. But the smoke from that bomb couldn't tear up an eye like listening to Bob and Elwood tell stories about growing up in Screven.

Hard to say what Bob's father would have thought upon hearing these tales since he had been gone for four years. Bob might have gotten another whuppin' had his father been alive, but I'd guess his mother never found out. If she had, she would have chastised Bob, then she would have turned her head and stifled her grin.

After he graduated, he could barely wait to get off the farm. At 17 years of age, he finally talked his mother into giving him permission to join the service, and while she wanted to, she knew she could not stop him. So, he gave up the freedom of a farm for a bunk in a barracks to quench his thirst for education. He had been a handful, he told me, full of the anger of grief from his father's passing when he was 13, complicated by teenage hormones that added more fuel to his anger. But his mother loved him. She wanted him to be happy, so according to Bob, she finally consented knowing he would have a "roof over his head, food to eat, and a boss." She knew he could manage his own behavior, because she and his father had taught him the importance of respect. "Yes, Sir!" was a phrase he knew how to say.

She also knew when he got settled, her son would continue to help her and his two sisters. And he did. Bob made $75.00 a month in the service. He sent all of it home to his mother and sisters. As he tells it, when buddies went to town on a Saturday night, he laundered their clothes for extra money. He did laundry and showered at the same time. He was never poor. He just didn't have cash. Some forty years later, he bought her a little house, right in downtown Screven just one block from her church.

When his mother finally gave him her support to join the Air Force, and the time drew near for him to be sworn in, he boarded that long train to Columbia, South Carolina. And when he did, he took all that his parents had taught him: respect for hard work and education; the meaning of honesty; and a strong sense of loyalty to his family and his God. He took neighborhood memories of playing in a river, sliding down a donkey's neck, and jinxing a principal's car in a way that would test a sense of humor more than a sense of disdain. But most of all, when Bob left Screven he took his sense of integrity, a sense of integrity that set him apart from others, integrity that was rich even for a young man with no means.

The Dance of Kindness
September 1998

"Jeanette, I couldn't do this for my mother. I can do it for yours." It was nine months after we married when Bob sat on the blue bedspread next to me and made this offer. His gaze was direct as he set his muscular hand on mine. "She should be with us."

I knew what he meant. His mother had lived in Georgia while he lived in California. He had been good to her. She loved the home he had bought her. She always had adequate money to live comfortably, but when she could no longer live alone, she moved in with his sister. Bob would have loved to have had her in California, but it was too far away from her community, her friends and her many family members, so he flew the continent repeatedly to spend what time he could with her before she died. His devotion was sincere, his loyalty powerful. We don't get do-overs in life. He knew that.

We sat quietly for a moment. We loved living in this house. We loved the bedroom view of the valley below and the mountains against the sky. We loved the cream colored, fluffy carpet, bordered with warm, wood flooring. But we adored the privacy as we melted into our new love. We were married in that house, downstairs under a beautiful arch fashioned of flowing white fabric and exquisitely adorned with flowers. Mother had walked me down the stairs, slowly, carefully, one step at a time. She was tiny, hunched over at the shoulders from life's female change, but she smiled each step, each pace.

"Are you sure, Bob?"

"Yes, I am. Your mother is wonderful, and she is not getting the care she needs. Bring her to live with us. You won't get this opportunity again. Life is not a dress rehearsal, Babe."

* * *

That was twelve years ago, twelve amazing years of watching my husband and my mother dance with tender words and affectionate play. The dance has always been one of kindness, mutual respect, and gentle wit. She would have done anything for Bob.

During those years, he did not provide the personal care Mother required, but he washed her car, changed the oil, and always watched for wear on her tires. He did all the grocery shopping, and kept the refrigerator stocked for all of us, and Mother's caregivers as well.

When it was time for him to retire, we packed up and moved to the desert, stuffed both our offices into one and gave Mother the extra bedroom only to find she was prone to melt in 110-degree weather. While she melted, Bob failed at retirement. He was happiest helping people, working with doctoral students, acting as a sage for CEOs. So, we packed up and moved again. He never complained.

* * *

Each morning, Miss Elma, as Bob called his mother-in-law, would sit at the kitchen table, coffee cup in hand, and read the newspaper with Bob. After being with us for a couple of years, I had difficulty getting Mother to bathe as her dementia slowly progressed. Daughters telling mothers to bathe is against the natural order of the world, tipping generational relationships upside down. She would have bathed had Bob asked, but his breeding was Southern to the core and such a request would have been undignified, a startling lack of respect. It was my job, my task, but I had yet to understand thoughts born of dementia.

One day, I prepared a bath for Mother upon rising, and presented her with an idea, an opportunity to look nice at the breakfast table when she had breakfast with Bob. She did not consent with words, but simply climbed in the bathtub. From that day forward, she was bathed, hair combed and lips carefully sculpted with red lipstick each morning in adequate time to have breakfast with her son-in-law.

* * *

He protected his mother-in-law, providing gentle nudging when she needed it. Before she moved in, Mother had developed a difficult attraction to alcohol, hiding in its haze from the physical pain she endured. She needed help controlling it, support from those around her, with love and boundaries to break the habit. One evening the three of us went out to dinner. Mother ordered wine.

The waitress I quietly cornered consented to cutting Miss Elma's wine with water. When it arrived, my petite-sized mother took a sip that was more reminiscent of a sizable swallow, pinky held high. She set the glass down, then announced, "This wine is as smooth as water." She looked at Bob and asked, "Would you like to try it?"

She pushed her glass across the table; Bob picked it up, brought it to his lips and took a sip. Surprised by the watered down flavor, he looked carefully at the glass in his hand. "Why Elma, I think this wine is…" Before he could speak further, I slapped his thigh under the booth. Startled, he paused, smiled, then continued, "…this wine is, um, well, Miss Elma, you are right. This wine is as smooth as water."

She always shared her glass of wine with Bob. He always took big sips so hers would be small.

Years later, it was Bob who witnessed the caregiver, a here-to-for trusted woman who had lived with us for five years, make Mother the target of her own emotional issues. Mom had fallen asleep at the breakfast table, head slumped forward half-way to her plate. Bob watched as the caregiver stood behind Mother, wrapped her arm around the front of Mother's face and snapped her fragile neck back against her own chest, forcing Mom's glasses against her face and blackening her eyes. He was angry. The caregiver was fired.

* * *

His affection for Miss Elma grew as the years passed. It was the same for her. Knowing she could never lose her daughter's love, she treated her son-in-law with a special deference. She would sit at the table and listen intently to the two of us, sometimes sparring over a current event, sometimes discussing the price of eggs. The topic never really mattered to her. Her comment was always the same.

"Jeanette, dear, can't you see that Bob is right?"

In the early years, I refrained from laughing out loud, smiling only silently as though fearful of reinforcing this behavior. Bob would nod his head, and in his genteel manner say with a slight Southern drawl, "Why thank you, Miss Elma."

Over time, maintaining decorum was impossible. One day, Bob and I were discussing a topic about which neither of us knew much. It could have been thermonuclear dynamics. As the questions and comments flew between us, we paused momentarily. It was a brief moment, but long enough for Mom to interject herself into a topic of which she knew nothing. Zip. Nada. Didn't matter.

She looked straight at me, and in her most lady like voice said, "Jeanette, dear, can't you see that Bob is right?" Her eyes were wide showing a sly touch of mirth, just enough to betray herself. I began to laugh.

"She always agrees with you, Bob!"

He leaned back in his chair, his laughter uncontrolled, his eyes tearing as he attempted to compose himself just enough to pay homage to this woman he loved like his own blood.

"Miss Elma," he said as he slapped his knee, "I couldn't ask for a better mother-in-law."

If she could talk today, able to compose whole sentences in her ailing mind, she would be the first to tell anyone willing to listen she could not have asked for a better son-in-law.

* * *

I won on both counts, but I am losing the wars raging in front of me. She is failing day-by-day, less responsive verbally, her body more taut and rigid. Bob's white count climbs steadily in spite of the chemo infusions. My auto-immune diseases continue to escalate causing my daily pain to explode. But my concern for my husband presses on me with such weight, I know I must make good use of the time we have. I must tell him all I feel before I have no time at all.

So, at night when his body is bone-tired from disease and the chemicals dripped in his veins, he lies on the bed, me kneeling beside him, and we talk about the meaning of death. We talk about love. We talk about gratefulness.

"Bob, I don't know if I ever thanked you."

"For what, Babe?"

"For letting my mother live with us. I just can't tell you how much it meant to me to have Mom here. I will always be grateful for everything you have done for her. You have been an amazing son-in-law."

"She deserved it, Babe. She's a wonderful person. What I couldn't do for my mother, I was able to do for yours. Like I always say, life's not a dress rehearsal."

As I kneel at his side, watching his blue eyes mist, I take his hand in mine. As we listen to the silence, my mind retraces my mother's words.

"Jeanette, dear, can't you see that Bob is right?"

Never Too Late
2008

Mother has bonded with Bob. Most people do, but Bob is the man who watches over her, in some ways a safe replacement for her long-deceased husband—at least, until she fell in love with Paul.

I cannot wait to tell the story. I dial my special friend, Sherri.

"Guess what, Sherri? Mother has a boyfriend! Well, a man friend. Well, I'm not sure what to call him. But his name is Paul." My 81-year-old mother has love spilling out of her heart. My friend listens, her voice cracks then she quietly declares, "With all the pain your mother has had in her life, finding love at her age is proof there is a God."

He lives across the street and two doors down. Mother could toss a softball to him, save the number of vulnerable windows in the neighborhood. On days when this shy man's courage is strong enough to absorb all her attention, he comes knocking on our door, sharing his front-teeth-missing ear-to-ear smile.

"Oh! You're home! I wasn't sure anyone was here. I was over earlier, but no one answered." I know what Paul will be wearing. He favors constancy, regularity. He dons a white straw Panama hat to hide his scalp, which his fine, sparse hair refuses to cover. His shirt is a standard white, a cotton blend, and he adorns it with his Naval pin on the left side directly above his pocket. His United States flag pin is always on the right. At his age, he does not have much interest in ties, but each day he sports his multi-colored inlaid gold bola tie. It would not be fitting for Paul to miss these adornments in his daily attire; he is too much of a gentleman.

Each time I see this man, a smile crosses my lips. "Oh, I was just out running some errands, Paul. Mom and the caregiver were probably asleep or on a walk. Come on in."

He is more than a neighbor. He is a soul who sees past Mother's angled little body that cannot stand straight, cannot look up at the stars unless she accomplishes a litany of activities like scrunching her knees down, setting her hands on her thighs to steady herself, tilting her rounded shoulders and neck back far enough to look up. Paul sees interminable sweetness. Miss Elma is his friend. He could be a rattlesnake, and I would kiss him for the kindness he shows my mother.

* * *

She met Paul some months ago during one of her numerous daily walks up and down the tree-lined hill as her little size six shoes ground down the cement sidewalk. My mother's caregiver, Lila, a rotund woman with long, black hair, mentioned the burgeoning connection one day. Curious, I joined them on a walk to witness, first-hand, this growing affection. When the three of us approached Paul's residence, he opened his front door and had it not been for his advanced age, I would have sworn before a jury there was a skip in his step as he came out to greet Mother.

"Well hello, Little Lady!" Mom never could resist a warm smile—with or without teeth—and left to her own will, she might have passed on putting her own teeth in daily, but Lila always made sure Elma was color coordinated, hair combed, and color on her cheeks. Her teeth were the final complement.

Paul stood there on the sidewalk, right foot forward, left hip slightly cocked, as he began telling his life's stories.

"You know, I died during the war. A Korean found me and left me for dead. I think it was the Brits that got me to Hong Kong, but I was dead. They brought me back in the hospital where they do all the research. You know, the one where all those vets are. Oh well, I can't remember. It doesn't matter anyway. I'm alive now." His war stories battled against each other, mixing bits of confusion with facts. As a veteran of two wars, he had the right to forget.

* * *

Each day she sees him, Elma listens to Paul. Her memory tries to hold on to the first part of his words so she can connect them to the last, and not lose the meaning in between. Mother offers a nod here and there, a smile or two, as she peers into his face as though gently touching his cheek. It is the minimalist chat a dementia patient can offer, but it is delivered with care and concern. She has not lost all her social graces. She has not lost her compassion. It is her mind that is slowly being erased. If anyone would ask her to explain what she had just heard, she would sputter, stall, and hunt for words with a creased brow and haunted look on her face. Bob and I do not ask her to try to explain, nor did Paul.

It takes him a couple visits to master Mother's name, as his mind can still hold memories. She is not as successful, so she calls him "Sweetheart." The very word causes a grimace as Paul inches his shoulders up to his ears as if he were a turtle trying to retract his head into his neck. In her daughter's presence, Paul is shy like a young child. My mother is not.

* * *

42

One day, as Elma walked by Paul's house, he nimbly approached her as she pushed her walker along the sidewalk. His words danced as he saw the bright red lipstick painted across her small, thin lips.

"Well, look at you! You've got your lips on! You look kissable." Paul meant it as a harmless compliment, but he gave it to a slightly reckless innocent betrayed by the playful wrinkles cradling her brown eyes. Her curved, shrunken spine tried to straighten as she reached her face toward his. Miss Elma seemed to want to look Paul in the eye.

"Well, what do you want me to do, kiss you?" She proceeded to pucker up as she patiently waited for a kiss. Paul's cheeks flushed, but he bent down and complied. It was a simple kiss—a brief encounter of two sets of aging lips—but it launched this tender friendship. She began to look forward to those kisses. On days when Mother could not stand tall enough to reach Paul's face, she would kiss the back of his hand leaving enough of her red lipstick to create the illusion of paint tenderly applied to his weathered skin.

Once the kisses started, the gentleman with the Navy pin and the bola around his collar, began knocking at the door toting gifts of chocolate that, in his mind, brought the etiquette of his generation to their home. The house filled up with chocolate until it finally eroded the will power I had worked so hard to build for so many years. Chocolate bars with almonds, or toffee, chocolate kisses, and when he ran out of chocolate, he honored Miss Elma with a plant or a box of cold cereal. Paul never came without a gift for her. She never failed to listen to him. He did not seem to mind that, for the most part, all Miss Elma could do well was listen.

As the visits increase, the neighbors notice. All of them had seen Mother on one of her walks, pushing her walker, stomping on fallen leaves with a kind of dementia-induced compulsion, smiling each step of the way. One day, as I open the door to greet Paul, the neighbors look at me with grins skipping across their faces as they silently mouth words, and throw excited hand signals behind his back as if to query, "Elma has a boyfriend?"

"Come on in, Paul," I tell him, then direct him with a wave of my arm toward the family room. As he walks through the front door, I glance back at the neighbors turning my thumbs-ups, containing my growing impulse to dance with excitement, wave my arms in the air and yell, "Yes! Mother has a boyfriend!"

In her earlier years, her mind was so quick her deep brown eyes would light up like twinkling lights on a Christmas tree. One could only wonder what would be left after Mom's ability to think, to plan, to reflect dissipated as her mind slowly drowned from the dementia. Then I watch Mother's face as Paul walks in the room. The tiny shell of a woman glows in a different way, and I realize what remains: pure heart, pure soul. Through her life, Mother had fine-tuned the art of giving love. This time, she was being loved. Miss Elma's warmth could have caused global warming on its own.

I retreat up the stairs to my office where piles of paperwork await me. Yet the girl inside is so curious, she wants to sneak into the family room to get a glimpse of how people in their eighties court, one with dementia, the other with memory challenges. I know conversation must be limited. Physical contact, too, I suppose, until I remember the stories about physical romance and dementia. At the thought, the little girl inside transforms into a parent as I slip down the stairs, feet barely touching the fibers of the carpet. Entering the family room from behind the couch, I find Mother and Paul sitting side-by-side, shoulders touching, his hand placed tenderly over hers, as their eyes focus on the television. The tenderness between them floats in the room like a warm mist.

"Hi, Mom. Hi, Paul." Paul unlatches his hand from Miss Elma's, jumps off the end of the couch, and stumbles for words like a kid caught in some kind of mischief. But there is no mischief. None at all. I simply ruin their ambience.

"Oh, Jeanette!" The elderly gentleman shifts his weight from one foot to the other. It is hard to ascertain whether the 86-year-old is trying to keep his balance or if he shuffles his feet from shyness. He stands there, his face taking on a reddish hue. "Your mother and I are just good friends." He is embarrassed—for holding her hand.

"Oh, I know, Paul. It's great Mother has a friend. She has family and caregivers, but since she moved in with my husband, Bob, and me, you have been the only friend she's had who is her age."

"I don't know how we became such good friends, but we really like to talk."

"I know. Mother enjoys talking with you."

He reaches into his pocket to retrieve his wallet. Paul's weathered hands sort through his cards, selecting one with tattered edges and a dusty brown color. He hands it to me. It is his military card.

"I'm a veteran of two wars. I believe in God and my country. I'm Catholic and I don't believe in hurting people. I'd never hurt your mother." Now, Miss Elma's daughter is in love with this spindly, old man, too.

"Oh, I know you would never hurt Mom, Paul." I believe this man would protect Mother's heart, but wonder if a well-intended hug would snap a rib in her badly osteoporotic frame. Parents of parents worry about all kinds of things.

"Well, you know, when your mother and her caregiver walked by my house one day, we just started talking. I guess that's how we became such good friends."

"That's so nice, Paul. Why don't you sit down and continue your visit?" He nods, then clasps his hands behind his back and pauses briefly.

"Does your mother ever go out to dinner?"

Take her on a date? I glance at Mother sitting on the couch with her eyes focusing on the television. As the daughter-turned-parent, I look at Mother's suitor, my mind bursting with jumbled thoughts as I realize I have not considered the consequences of their hearts becoming entwined. What if Mother needs to use the bathroom? I know she cannot manage that alone. Does Paul ever become confused while driving? What are his driving skills like at his age? All my questions lead to a solitary answer of "No."

"She doesn't really go out to dinner, Paul." As a daughter, I hate being a parent to a parent when I have to use the word "no."

"Oh, okay." There is silence as his shoulders fall, and the hope drains from his expression like a wave disappearing back into an ocean. "Well, I really need to be going now, anyway. You'll be having dinner soon." He turns his face toward Miss Elma. "I should go home now."

"Okay, Sweetheart."

Paul's ears turn a mild crimson hearing this. "Oh, you shouldn't call me that."

"Why not? I'll call you Sweetheart if I want to." Mother does not stop there. She stands up to get kissed. She collects kisses, like she collects stuffed toys, each one getting special attention. Paul steps back, and his grey, fluid eyebrows curve up his forehead. He has been known to solicit a kiss or two from this woman, but not in front of her daughter, the same daughter he painstakingly tried to reassure seconds ago.

"Well, Paul, no one can leave without a kiss goodbye from Mom. She's just that kind of person." Mother is still standing, stretching up to Paul, and waiting for her kiss. She does not always remember a grandchild's name, or a daughter-in-law's name, but she does not forget she is waiting for this kiss. The old gentleman sees there is no avoiding it, so he leans over and gives Miss Elma a quick kiss on the lips.

As I walk him to the door, he whispers in my ear, "What is your mother's name again?" Sometimes love requires no memory.

At times, Paul admits he becomes disoriented now and then, but he shrugs his lean shoulders, smiles, and says, "Well, at 86, I'm not doing so bad." It is true. His war stories are sometimes hard to follow until, with the persistence of a detective, I dig deep with questions to understand what, "I died, but came back again," really means. Paul was left for dead on a beach in Korea, picked up by the Brits and taken to Hong Kong. And while he shows us his purple heart, the exact circumstances of the brave act that won him this award continues to evolve. It is a story in the telling.

Although Mother can always focus on Paul's face, she cannot always concentrate on his stories. Sometimes it is due to dementia. Sometimes a fog sets in her eyes from the haze of affection she feels for this man.

"Are you married?" she asks him one day when she and her caregiver are out methodically traipsing up and down the hills. Paul must have meandered around her comment, but he chose to share her question with me.

"You know, your mother asked me if I was married."
"Did she?"

47

"When my last wife died, several widows asked me to dinner. Oh, I wasn't interested. It hasn't been a year yet since my wife died. I still miss her." He makes his point.

"Well, Paul," I calibrate my voice to a tone I hope will sound soothing. "I wouldn't worry about Mom's question. She doesn't mean anything by it. Sometimes, she still thinks she is married to my dad."

Mom remembers Dad, but does not remember him suddenly falling at her feet, hitting the floor of their bedroom. With his heart attack erased from her mind, Elma is left with brief memories of marriage. She had been married to a man dead for fifteen years by the time she met Paul. But her question makes him skittish like a nervous cat, and he quits visiting. Mother notices less than her daughter as the weeks pass by.

* * *

"Hey, Paul!" I toss my greeting out the window of my car, and slow my engine to speak to him. He is wearing the same clothes, the same hat, sporting the same smile. He rummages through the back seat of his aging tan car which appears as if it would fail to start even if someone released the brakes and chased it downhill. On the seat sat a dozen or more chocolate bars the manager at the local grocery store had given Paul. I guess much of it was past its expiration date, and covered with cream-colored speckles. Sometimes the chocolate given to this spritely, old gentleman had turned color throughout and crumbled apart in grainy little pieces. Age does that to chocolate, and while I am able to discard his aging chocolate gifts, I cannot let go of this aged man. Like his chocolate, he owns a piece of my mother's heart; a piece of my own, as well.

"We miss seeing you, Paul!" This is not the first time his ears have heard this. "Why don't you come over and visit?" He gives me a long list of things he must get done: visit the VA Center in Long Beach, take chocolate to the kids in school, maybe even see a dentist. He offers another wide grin, and points to his teeth, verification he still needs new dentures. As the days pass, he seems to forget Mother had asked him if he was married. Or perhaps he responds to my frequent urgings. The reason will never be known, but one afternoon there comes a tapping at the door. I open it to find Mother's personal Candy Man.

He chats, laughs, and seems to blend into the home like a worn piece of furniture that belongs in the room. Miss Elma's birthday is near, so I invite Paul to a small celebration in honor of her day, but he glances at the floor. "Well, I'm not sure what I'll be doing that day." He delivers his words in quick stops and starts. "I'm going to have company for Mother's Day, you know."

"It's so nice you have company coming. How long are they staying?"

"Until Sunday."

"Well, that's great news. Mom's birthday is the day after Mother's Day."

"Oh." He shifts his lean body, and touches his arm to his forehead as though lifting small beads of sweat off his skin. "Well, you never can tell what might happen between now and then." His hesitance does not dissuade me. I handwrite an invitation with the date and time, and hand it to Paul.

"Here, if you can make it, we'd love to have you join us for Mother's birthday dinner." What I failed to say is we will remind him so he cannot forget.

Yet, I have forgotten something. Something quite important. You see, some of Mother's behaviors have become those of a young child, an age when eating with one's hands makes sense. Dementia controls the calendar so the compromised brain travels back in time. I begin to pace and fret, posing questions to myself. How would Paul respond if he sees Mom arrange the food on her plate into systematic shapes and patterns? What if she licks her spoon clean so she can see her reflection in it? Or her plate? Will he stop calling on her? Mother's obsession is to over clean. My obsession is to over help.

Paul arrives with a two-pound box of candy, a bottle of wine, with three large chocolate bars bound together by a white lace wedding garter, another free gift, he explains, from the manager of the grocery store. His white shirt is adorned with his standard bola, a blue blazer, and his Panama hat. A military pin on his coat sparkles with small diamonds. He looks like a Navy man who has misplaced his dentures. Miss Elma's eyes danced at the sight of him. And when they do, I know I cannot imagine a more handsome suitor for my mother.

"Well hello there, Elma!" He remembers her name.

When it is time to eat, I seat Paul beside Mother, and directly across from Bob. I know Paul's eyes will focus on Bob, and not on my mother. The orchestrated seating arrangement makes me feel oddly disloyal to Mom, but it prevents the beads of sweat I expected on my own forehead. Mother's whole focus is eating. Everyone else does all the talking.

While Miss Elma eats the dinner she so carefully arranges, we listen to Paul's war tales. Because I know his memories would eventually evaporate, I build my own mental filing cabinet and listen carefully to his words. He served in World War II and Korea, had been commended for his intelligence work, kissed by Eleanor Roosevelt and presented with a purple heart. It seems Paul had seen so much in life, he was a treasure, but I knew he was a treasure waiting to be forgotten. Once lost, old memories cannot be found again.

After the cake was eaten, the party moves into the family room. Paul sits with Mother's hand in his, leaving his other hand free to punctuate his stories when the need to animate strikes him. Most of his comments are directed to Bob and me. Mother sits and smiles. Paul is holding her hand.

Lila notices Mother's eyes are beginning to close, her head listing to one side. "Miss Elma, you are getting sleepy." Lila's English had a faint accent of Spanish with the singsong rhythm of Tagalog. She speaks all three, but the Tagalog of the Philippines was her native tongue.

"Elma, my dear, you are getting sleepy. It's our bedtime. We need to go to bed."

"No!" Mother's voice is normally peaceful, even playful. Not now. "I'm *not* tired, and I'm *not* going to bed!"

Mother looks up at Paul, her expression reminiscent of a 1950's teenager being serenaded by Elvis. Paul smiles, looks down at her and says, "Elma, I'm sorry. I have stayed too long."

Miss Elma does not want her boyfriend to leave, but Paul continues.

"I should go home. You're tired, Elma. You need to go to bed." He pats her arm gently. "I need to go home, because I need to go to bed, too."

The pause is, oh, so short. Then in a tiny voice my tiny mother asks a very big question.

"You want to go to bed with me?"

I manage to avoid spraying my just-sipped tea into the air, but could not stop my rolling laughter. Bob begins to slap his thighs as tears brim in his dancing blue eyes. Lila bends over, her hands on her knees while she convulses with rapid giggles. The three of us have simply lost all sense of decorum.

Paul's blue eyes grow as round as two basketballs, and his bushy eyebrows arch to the sky with this surprise offer. The old gentleman shifts on the couch, stalling, contemplating how to best address the situation. Miss Elma sits peacefully. She pays us no mind, ignoring our laughter. She is happy holding Paul's hand.

He finally looks at her face and smiles. "I guess things have changed a lot since the old days." Elma and Paul own the only dignity in the room.

In spite of Mother's offer, or perhaps because of her offer, this gentle man returns again and again, each time with some kind of treat in hand. Sometimes it is more chocolate. Sometimes it is grape juice. Sometimes it is cold cereal with bits of marshmallows in shapes and colors that would attract most any child's attention, even the 81-year-old mother-turned-child who lives with her daughter. But the biggest treat of all was that warm, front-teeth-gone grin.

I Can't
August 2010

I can't do it. I just can't. Reality descends upon me, causing
an exhalation large enough to be heard in the next room. I
am hiding in bed this morning, late in rising, eyes closed as
my mind wanders. I am tormented as I struggle with
thoughts of a husband with cancer and a mother with
dementia. We still live together. I care for him. I manage
care for her.

Bob is brave as he steadies himself for his
upcoming chemo treatments. Mother is brave as she faces
dementia with surprising grace even in her childlike state. I
am not. Not today. Today I am frightened by what lies
ahead. I am frightened of having arthritis, fibromyalgia,
neuropathy and Crohn's all attacking my body with
unending pain that burns both day and night. But my pain
feels insignificant compared to my fear of failing the people I
love the most, in the biggest way, in the deepest way.

I can't do it. Even lying under the sheets, I cannot
seem to hide from the truth. During the last few months only
one of Mother's caregivers has performed. One sat in a
chair as though providing care implied chatting endlessly
about nothing. One sat outside, cell phone glued to her ear,
while her patient was left unattended. Others, edging up in
years, left stoves lit, refrigerators open, and medications in
disarray. It seemed as though I terminated someone's
employment weekly.

Mother has been with us for twelve years now. Each
morning "Miss Elma" and Lila, her live-in caregiver, sit at the
glass table set with various colored napkins which rarely
match, and old pink placemats, placemats that were ready

to be discarded by my sister-in-law before my pink-loving mother rescued them.

The tradition continues as Mother has breakfast with Bob. He always greets her with a grin that deepens his dimples. Mom, even with diminishing mental capacities, always had a flair for humor. One night about ten years ago, when the three of us were at dinner with friends, I mentioned to Bob we should pay for two-thirds of the dinner since Mother was with us. Our friend, Harry, interrupted. "Absolutely not! I want to pay for half of Elma's dinner."

Mom looked at Harry, then sat up, head held high, looked at me and said, "If this man pays for half of my dinner, am I obligated?" The whole restaurant must have heard our laughter. Back then, her comments reflected complex humor. Now her jokes are compressed into playful one-liners to accommodate her dementia. When I tease her, she looks at me with a sly grin, then tells me, "Shut up, Jeanette," and I cackle like a little kid. As her abilities decrease, she never misses on timing. She warms people like an Olympic flame, always burning, always bright. For Bob and me, she warmed our kitchen while making us laugh.

* * *

I won't make it. I pull the bed covers down, and curse the ceiling. *I can't do it!* I can't take care of both of them and me, too. But he is my husband, and she is the mother who sometimes calls me, "Mommy." He gave her twelve years of our thirteen years of marriage by inviting her into our home. He has cancer. It is his turn for my focused attention. Mother will have to leave.

I remember her story, the story that revealed so much about her childhood. She was little, maybe six or seven years of age. Her parents were unable to communicate past their mutual anger, unable to reignite the love that had been stomped out like old embers. So they built a house of quiet, so quiet they spoke only when necessary to pass a plate of food at the dinner table, or to complete a household project that took four hands instead of two. My grandparents loved their daughter, but showing it required communicating, a habit which died by the time my mother was four. One day, she walked home from school early to find the house empty. Her father worked, and her mother had stepped out. Little Elma cried tears a small child should not have to cry. Convinced her parents had moved away and left her, she ran to the neighbors and wept uncontrollably. She was wrong. They had not left, and her parents did love her. But as she tried to make sense of their quiet behaviors, this small child assumed the burden of guilt for her parent's unhappiness, then built her own explanations in her young mind, creating a story of words that did not fit.

Now, after twelve years of caring for her, I must do the unthinkable, the absolute unbearable. I must find a facility, a substitute home that can do for my mother what I no longer can.

I interview six locations by phone. I inspect three looking for dirty carpets, floors with rugs that could trip feet no longer able to step, but shuffle instead. I ask about medication management, caregiver-to-patient ratios, the level of nursing care provided. I want to know if they will walk her so she will keep her balance. I want to know if they will let her sit with the patients who can talk and interact with her, if caregivers and other staff will do the same. I expect a lot. They promise a lot. They promise so much I finally feel comfortable and make my selection.

In the evening I take Mom outside and we sit, hand-in-hand, swinging on our porch swing, looking at the trees, listening to the birds.

"Mom, I need you to help me with something." She looks at me, smiles, and nods her head. "Bob is sick, Mom. He has cancer, and he needs to have treatments." She listens to my words with sadness on her face. "I need to take care of him. I need for you to stay in a place, like a little hotel, where they can help you while I help him. Will you do that for me?"

She needs repetition for the information to hold in her mind, so every evening for five nights we sit on the swing, and I ask for her help. Each evening she tells me the same thing. "I can do that if it helps, Jeanette." Each evening my heart dies a little more, like a sunflower wilting from lack of water with no sun to follow across the sky.

I never make it sound permanent, like a period at the end of a sentence, or the death of a firefly as its glow goes out forever. *I can't.* I want Bob well and Mom home. I want my family together in our tidy house, with all the shelves straight, the furniture in place, with refrigerators and blenders humming in the kitchen. But life does not care what I want. It has trapped me in a world of competing unkindnesses: I must remove my mother from the home where she feels safe to provide my husband a private place to die. There are no wins, it seems. Only losses.

It is time to take her for a visit to this "hotel" facility, hopefully a visit where she meets one of the many pets roaming the halls and fraternizing with patients. Perhaps Mother will not notice the residents are at various levels of mental decline. Some seem almost normal, but others wander without direction, yell out, or withdraw into a private world. Mother walks in the front door, I introduce her to some of the staff I have met, and she pets the dog.

"Let's go." She does not even twist her rounded shoulders up to look up at me. She is done. She senses the doors keep the residents locked in, and she will not leave the foyer, or walk down the hall. "Let's go." And so we leave.

Friday arrives, the day the facility is expecting her, and I wonder just how is it I am able to do this? How can I drive this incredible woman to a locked brick facility, then turn around and leave her? How do I leave my mother at a strange place where people roam the halls, so many unable to make sense of their own worlds? How do I give up this woman who has become my child? *I can't.* I swear to God, I can't.

I dress her in one of her prettiest pink outfits. I brush her cheeks with a pink glow. Her eyes usually dance when she sees pink. Today they barely move. I pencil in her eyebrows, and put on her lipstick, pick up her brush and begin to brush her hair. She knows where she is going today. Her bags are packed, her pink bedding already boxed.

"Mom, I think you are going to make some good friends." I try to smile while she sits so quietly. My words change nothing. She looks up into my face.

"Can I ask you something?"

"Of course you can, Mom." A tear drops off her cheek as she looks into my eyes. She pauses. With an unsteady lower lip, she asks me a question in a timid voice.

"Do you still love me?"

I do not ask her why she asks this, because I know, and if I die this moment, this very minute, it will have been too late – too late to protect this child before me from feeling the fear that another parent is going to abandon her.

"Oh God, Mother, I love you so much. I will always love you. There is nothing you could do to make me stop loving you. Nothing." I reach down and kiss the pink on her cheek. I try so hard not to cry, not to make this even more painful for her. My heart feels so much my mind stalls and lapses into meaningless conversation.

"I think you are going to like the dogs that live there. The big one really seemed to like you." She tries to smile. She, too, senses our internal worlds cannot be disclosed. This pain cannot be laid open in words between us. Doing so could cause cracks in our very souls.

The caregiver packed the car, heaving suitcases and bedding into the trunk. When we arrive, I watch Mother's response. Our roles reverse, as she forces a smile to make my world easier. She always had more concern for her children than for herself.

The drive home leaves my mind unattended, save freeway traffic. When did she become my child? Was it when she could not select clothes for a trip to town beyond a ragged housecoat? Was it when she could no longer use a fork as her hands trembled? Or was it the first time she called me, "Mommy?" I never had a child until my mother became one, and so she taught me how to love selflessly, first as my mother then as my child.

Through the weekend, I hide my tears from my husband, but they flow with a pain I could not have imagined as though I just gave my child up for adoption, just gave her to someone else, to someone else who cannot give her the love I gave her. I gave to a company, a damn organization for God's sake! But for now, they can give her the care I cannot: the feeding, the dressing, the bathing.

The tears finally slow by Monday morning, the first day of Bob's chemo. It is time for me to get up, dress, and drive my husband to his infusion, but I lie in bed hiding under my closed eyelids.

I can't do it! I just can't.

But I do.

White Ceiling
October 2010

My Love,

I truly feel I have at last met my soul mate in life which arouses in me a sense of spirituality I have never experienced before. To think of this truly brings tears.

Robert Canady, May 20, 1995

I want to talk, but my voice is mute, my lips still. When I do try, Bob's anger steams off his shoulders, and his eyes glare. Last year his temperament began to change. I noticed he was bone tired at times. He insisted he napped more because he could, because retirement gave him that privilege. I had no reason to doubt his explanation. But neither of us could see the road ahead. Even if we could have, there were no detours left to take.

I wonder now if this change was influenced by the cancer. Nothing pleased him. He walked out on conversations. With time, I tired of it, and yearned for the easy-going husband I had married. I caught his attention when I offered to buy him out of the house so he could move back to Georgia. He wanted to stay. He righted his attitude within what seemed like seconds. In spite of his response, I was slow to forgive as I stumbled over the arrogance of my own hurt.

* * *

Now, as he faces leukemia, I put the last of my anger in an imaginary basket, with a strong lid, one I can sit on, forcing it shut so the basket's contents cannot be released. I do not stop to consider the costs of stuffing emotion. I do not have the time. I am too consumed with worry my husband is dying. So, through the night I stare at the bedroom ceiling while he sleeps, and try to find my focus in a dimly lit room.

Morning comes quickly. It seems my gaze is still fixed on the white ceiling, as I contemplate what I have to accomplish today. I need to drive Bob to his doctor appointment, then the infusion center, leave him with the oncology staff, then go to the facility to check on Mother. I cannot tell who will die first.

I refocus my eyes on the benign ceiling. White space is like a psychiatrist with a neutral expression, like a blank canvas on which patients can paint many colors of emotion without fear of judgment. I would paint my unresolved anger red—bright red. My love would be blue, I guess. But if I closed my eyes, I fear other colors would fly off the palate creating colorific chaos, and nothing would match, and my ceiling would have no order at all. Things used to seem so clear, but now there are so many answers I cannot find.

As I shower and dress, I retrace past conversations, the hurtful type, the ones I should have forgotten. While rare, his comments could be curt and sharp enough to cut down a sizable tree. But the sting of such remarks are hard to erase from a mind, especially mine. I seize on such things, wrap them in a coating as hard as a walnut's shell, then stash them away for a blustery winter when I might need ammunition. One bad turn deserves another, I guess, yet these simple, stupid, petty comments we sometimes make can erode the love between two people as if being right is more important than protecting love.

* * *

Bob gets in the passenger side of the car, and I open the door to the driver's side. As we drive down the freeway, he dials his sister in his hometown. Then he calls his son in Florida. The conversations are good for Bob, but they give my mind time to pose questions that put pain in my heart. *Why is he so grumpy with me? Does he still love me?* God, how I would like to drive these thoughts into a ditch.

I try to steer my mind onto a different road. I remember the romance of the first year, deep, rich and hot. But nothing was as intense as the love that put fire in our intimacy. Now Bob watches TV, eats, goes back to the TV, switches to the Internet, then goes to bed. He does not tell me goodnight. He simply goes to bed. Before, we had evening walks outside, in a park, where we could see coyotes and rabbits and squirrels. Now, TVs, email and Facebook vie for his attention. Screens can be tough competition.

My routine has its own flaws. I finish the kitchen, check email, then start my evening exercise to control pain—the only treatment possible when one is allergic to pain medications. Do I start early enough to go to bed at 10:30 when my husband retires? No. Does he understand I am not rejecting him? I do not know. Maybe it takes the darkness of death to turn on the lights. *How dare he turn on the lights.*

We sit in the oncologist's small waiting room, made bigger only by the headcount of cancer patients, family members and caregivers. We do not sit long. Patients with scheduled chemo infusions get priority treatment.

"Bob Canady?" The oncology nurse glances around the shoulder-to-shoulder room in search of Bob as he stands and disappears with her behind the off-white door. He is weighed, blood pressure and pulse checked, blood drawn, then returned to the waiting room until an examining room is free. By now Bob's seat is gone, sacrificed for a woman so weakened by chemo allowing her to stand was unthinkable. When Bob returns, I give him my seat.

The oncologist sees us in one of the many compact examining rooms. He is a tall man, big enough to carry a large sized heart in his chest, big enough to carry the weight of many lives on his shoulders, mixing his concern with warm, straightforward words. I wonder how he is able to treat the hundreds of patients he sees each month. He does the same exam each time he sees Bob, taking care to not miss a single node that might be swollen, or a slight change in how Bob's lungs breathe in and exhale air. The doctor sits on the stool and gives us his full attention. He is smart. He is so smart we don't feel the need for multiple opinions. His reputation is so good we are certain he will know how to buy Bob time.

We drive to the infusion center, and Bob slowly opens his door, then disappears into the building. I drive down the street two miles, and park in the visitors parking at the assisted living community where I have placed Mother. Bob and I schedule our days to allow me the time to visit with her and feed her lunch. I walk in to find her slumped over in her chair with a dozen people who, when not blurting out unintelligible sentences, slump over and sleep themselves. It angers me to see her in this room when others, more functional, sit in a room down the hall, and are at least able to communicate with each other. When she is with them, she is more able to respond. She needs more stimulation. I need less. I feed her, talk with her, kiss her, then answer my phone. Bob's chemo is done and he is waiting for me to pick him up, so I leave. Yes, I need less.

When we arrive at the house, I quietly resolve we not slip into our regular habits. I know our evenings together are numbered. I have lost a spouse before. This is a routine of lost time, a loss that cannot be found again. There he sits glued to the TV, while I, like a two-year-old, want to walk to his big chair and kick him in the shins. But I can't kick anyone, least of all the man I love.

Tonight I am determined to change our behavior.

"You can't do that anymore, Bob." My smile carefully hides my frustration. I don't want to anger him. I am not afraid to piss him off, I just don't want to. He has leukemia.

"What can't I do?"

"You can't go to bed without kissing me goodnight." The very dimples that make me want him highlight the warmth of his smile.

And so, we reinstate a long lost kissing ritual. Still, I want more of him, so I make a recommendation.

"Bob, when you are done watching TV, looking at Facebook and email, why don't you stop by the workout room and we will watch something together?"

"Like what?" I look for a smile, wait for his dimples to show, but his face is still save the arched eyebrows. We both know he is a news and Fox junkie, and I think Fox is junk.

"I don't know. Why don't we find something we both like?" I know it will be a leap, but I am trying to have faith.

"Okay," he says, his expression subtle.

Nightfall puts our new routine in motion. Bob watches the TV, while I check email. He checks email, while I exercise. But tonight when he is done with the Internet, my husband quietly slips into the workout room and lies down on the couch behind me to watch TV. I turn around and see his grin, and realize there are no butterflies in the world that could flutter like the ones inside of me. We decide on a classic: All in the Family. Bob's whole body quakes with laughter as Archie Bunker yells at Meathead. I laugh as my husband chuckles, but mostly I laugh because he is in the room, *with me.*

"Well, Babe, I'm hitting the sack." He steps over to the treadmill, closes his eyes, and puckers up impishly, extending his lips toward mine. I bend forward and collect on our deal. As he walks out the door, I notice his steps are slow. He is tired, so tired. I give him time to undress, brush his teeth, and crawl into bed. I cannot stand being ten feet away from him tonight, so I slip into the room, and lie next to him on the bed. I want to turn on my side, and cuddle up to his tired body. I can't. I cannot lie on my side. My back and my neck are too full of pain from the multiple auto-immune disorders. *How can this be? My husband is dying and I can't hold him.*

He is exhausted from the harsh chemicals dripped into his veins today, circulating through his not-so-tough body. Inside our home, our walls, the courage that others see wanes. I hear the concern in the soft cadence of his voice. I see the timidity in his face. He shares his fears about dying, his fears about living with pain. I absorb his every word as I listen with my ears, my mind, my heart, knowing someday soon these moments will be no more. Then he pauses, and gently asks me a question.

"You know what I wish, Babe?" He reaches over and puts his hand on mine as we both look up at the white ceiling.

"No, Honey, I don't. What do you wish?"

He turns his face to look at me.

"I wish we had met 20 years earlier so we could have had 20 more years together." A silent tear falls down his cheek.

I take my hand from his, and cover my face as I start to cry. And I cry, and I cry. When I can stop, I sit up in bed so I can look into his eyes.

"I didn't know you felt that way. I didn't know." Tears stream down my face as I bury my head in my knees.

If only I had known. *Oh God, if only I had known.*

The Office Door
November 2010

"Oh damn." It hits me as I step out of our home office. I have inadvertently locked the door, and the only key sits inside resting comfortably on my desk. I jiggle the door handle hoping it will open, but it is locked tight and the door will not budge. This bonus room is our refuge, the place Bob and I spend most of our time each day and part of our evening as well. It is a perfect arrangement, and it is Bob's hideout during chemo weeks. Until today.

"How did you lock the key in the office?" Bob's upper lip is curling upward; the characteristic position it assumes during chemo week. My typically easy going husband transforms—into what I am not clear—but I know I do not recognize this species. This mood starts on day two of chemo week. He is on day four of five.

"Honey, I didn't mean to lock the door." If he were a bear, he would have already started to growl. Soon, very soon, he will begin to feel the absence of his daily drugs: email and Facebook. Lucky for me, we have to drive thirty miles to his two-hour infusion, a distraction from a locked office to be sure. But it is unlucky for him. He does not feel good about this transformation, this different "being" he becomes during chemo week.

While I dress, he picks at the door with unbent paper clips, then a knife, and finally escalates to a screwdriver.

"I can't get this damn door open. I've tried everything I can think of. I'm calling a locksmith." He stomps down the stairs in search of an archaic tool: a phone book.

He storms back up the stairs. While I dress he tells me the first locksmith cannot come to the house until tomorrow morning. The second one cannot come until tomorrow afternoon. The third one can make it at 4:30 today. I am relieved. He is just pissed. I am sure I watch his jaw muscles contract as though he is ready to gnash his teeth, but I wonder if my own irritation is not provoking my perceptions. As I adjust my bra, I adjust my attitude. After all, this is chemo week, and it has to be less fun for him than me. Perhaps.

We get in my old Lexus, and I back out of the garage. The quiet in the car communicates whole conversations. I can guess my husband is using curse words in the silence of his mind.

Not me. I am daydreaming about having an ejector seat installed on the passenger side of my car. I might gain a moment of joy watching Sir Grump catapult into space, but I love him and I know by tomorrow afternoon, the chemo will have a softer edge, my husband will be human again, and so for now, I will make sure his seat belt is clasped and tight. Guilt always did hold me tighter than anger.

It is 1:30 by the time we get back from chemo and lunch, a mere three hours from a date with a locksmith. Bob's addiction to email is beginning to resemble a junkie without a fix. I am standing in the hall next to the office when his need for e-drugs overwhelms him. He marches up the stairs, down the hall, right up to the locked office door.

It appears as though smoke is fuming from his nose and ears, but I am sure this is my imagination. He turns his body to the side, leans back, lifts his leg in the air, and cocks his ankle into position. He then kicks the door with the power of a small grenade blasting it open. Bob looks at the broken door, as though he has just become the victor in some holy battle.

"Jesus, Bob, you just broke the door! Why the hell did you do that?"

"Because the locksmith won't be here for three more hours. That's why!" Some facial expressions are beyond smug.

"That's just great. Now, we have to pay to have the door replaced."

"Well, now we won't have to pay the locksmith."

* * *

It is another tough week with the chemo. Bob's vein still accepts it with ease, and although tired after each infusion, we are relieved he has no physical side effects, but I can only imagine Bob's emotional experience is akin to sitting in a small sailboat in the midst of a hurricane.

"Dr. Miller," Bob starts his question as he sits on the examining table. The exam is complete, and we have a few fleeting moments to bring forward any questions we might have. "Is it possible this chemo could, well…" The pause is deliberate as my husband searches for the right words. "Is it possible someone might be a little moody on this chemo?"

Internally, I sigh a sizable sigh, if not the largest sigh of my life, but my expression does not change, my eyes do not widen, and my head does not roll. I am so relieved my husband is searching for answers.

Dr. Miller turns and looks at me, searching for any kind of clue. I am more than mute. I am impossible to decipher.

"Well yes, Bob, this chemo can cause moodiness." He points his finger at him. "But *you* do not need to put that on *her*," and he points the same finger at me. "You *need* her."

Bob sits with his legs hanging off the examining table, both arms folded against his large chest. "Well," he says stiffly, "it's not that bad, anyway."

Sometimes storms brew inside me, all hell breaking loose like a tornado ripping down a path. An onlooker might never know. Today is a bit like that, with an odd twist of humor, as I sit stoically attempting to control my inclination to slap Bob upside the head like an angry mother, or laugh uncontrollably at his comment as though he is a gifted comedian, but I love this man so much, I become the Mona Lisa, so still, so unreadable.

I just might reconsider the ejector seat, anyway.

Holding On
December 2010

A year ago he was complete, a whole operating system, a babe even at his 80th birthday party. I threw the party, but he drove the plan like a well-oiled Cadillac down to the black and white theme. His suit was raven, his white shirt had a subtle sheen that caught the glow of his candles, and his white tie was dotted with perfectly formed small black squares. Bob looked as if from a royal family, but his warmth and laughter was Southern to the core. To me, he was a babe.

He is still my babe—through the chemo, the pain, the chemically-induced mood swings, and anything else that comes with cancer or "for better or worse." Tonight, he ambles over to the couch, limbs sagging as though he is wilting before my eyes. He quietly lies down, remote in hand, and turns on the television. My husband is gearing up for another week of infusions.

I try to unwind as I clean the kitchen, moving pots and pans from one place to the next as though I am lost in the small room. My cell screen lights up diverting my attention away from the stack of dirty dishes. I recognize the number, and take off my wet kitchen gloves quickly so I do not miss the call. It is the nurse at the assisted living facility calling about my mother. Mom has a cold, it is going into her chest, her breathing is labored.

The facility nurses are reluctant to call me these days. They are concerned Mother's failing condition will add angst to my already stressed life. They know my husband has leukemia. I cannot split my love for each, like firewood under the pressure of an axe. Love is whole and organic, like a tree reaching up to the sky, like roots boring into deep, rich soil. My heart does not know any other way to love. It is the withholding of information by the nursing staff that increases the tension in my neck, shoulders and any muscle in my body not yet contracted. Not knowing makes me feel like a powder keg, with lit fuses attached to each limb.

Why did they not call before her breathing became labored? I bite my tongue in hopes of preventing an explosion. Having cared for my mother for twelve years, I know her complicated case better than any facility nurse. They need my input, but they wait too long to act. We all know for a woman in her weakened condition such symptoms are like a bell announcing an oncoming death. My answer is quick. "Call Dr. Bae, then call me back."

He is her primary care physician, an indispensable member of her care team. He plays the same role in our lives as well. Dr. Bae's commitment to patients is like a country doc, one who does not forget each patient is human, each unique, and each with a heart that needs to be touched. These days he is touching ours more than he could imagine.

He must have sensed Mother's hesitance during her first appointment eleven years ago. He asked her question after question recording her responses with one hand, while touching her arm with his other hand during the entire interview. She trusts him. I trust him. He trusts me. We have already exchanged cell numbers.

My cell screen lights up again. It is Dr. Bae.

"Hi, Dr. Bae. Calling about Mom?"

"Hi, Jeanette. Yes, I just got a call from the nurse at the facility. They are concerned Elma is getting weak and less responsive. She is having increased trouble breathing."

"I know. These symptoms started a couple of days ago, and they are getting worse." My tired body leans against the kitchen door jamb as I run my hand quickly through my short, graying hair. "I was in the facility Friday."

"What's your intuition on this? Do you want me to see her?"

"Well, it's not just that her breathing is a bit labored. You can hear the bronchial congestion. I think she will be into pneumonia soon. My intuition? I think she should be examined. Soon."

"I agree. I'll call the facility, and see her tomorrow morning."

"Dr. Bae, I can't make it tomorrow morning. Bob has an appointment at nine with the oncologist. After that, he has chemo."

"I've got it covered, Jeanette. I'll arrange for her to be brought to my office. You concentrate on Bob. I'll take care of Mom." It touches me he calls her Mom as though he has adopted her. My chest releases the air I was unconsciously holding.

"Thanks, Dr. Bae." I wonder what I would do without his support.

"I may need to admit her to the hospital, but as soon as I see her, I'll call you." I thank him again, and hang up my phone in time to hear the doorbell ring.

Keli, my as-close-as-you-can-get to an adopted little sister, is here. I met her some forty years ago when she was seventeen years old, light brown hair parted down the middle, creamy complexion spotted with an occasional adolescent blemish. She hardly spoke she was so shy. Her boyfriend, an acquaintance of mine, wanted me to meet her, so there she sat in the living room of an older twenty-four-year-old woman, timid and almost unable to speak. Ultimately, she ditched the boyfriend, but our friendship has continued for four decades.

Keli is between jobs and sweeps into town on chemo weeks during which we take turns switching from Mom to Bob and back again, from the chemo center to the facility, from the car to the house. With Keli I have two right hands. Without her my limbs feel brittle and stiff, dangerously close to snapping with one more responsibility regardless of size.

"Oh, God, I am so glad you are here."

"Well, I am!" She smiles and her fresh face beams. She needs to help as much as I need her help. I wrap both arms around her as she steps in the door.

"Prepare yourself, Keli. It's going to be a tough week."

Survival Does Not Allow It
December 2010

The morning comes quickly as I climb out from under the sheets, stepping lightly on the carpet so Bob can sleep longer. I head for my workout room, my quiet space, where my treadmill awaits. The inactivity of sleep builds arthritic pain and stiffness through the night as my auto-immune system attacks my tissues. Movement calms it. So I move— 90 minutes every morning when I get up and every evening before going to bed, seven days a week for the last 30 years. Exercise is my pain pill.

Keli meets me in the hall and we strategize the day. We need two cars today. Bob has his oncology appointment and chemo. We are unsure if Mother will be at the facility or in the hospital, so we finish breakfast and are cleaning the kitchen when my cell phone rings. The number is Dr. Bae's.

"How is she doing?" I do not even say hello, as if the conversation from last night simply continues.

"She doesn't sound good, Jeanette. I am sending her to the emergency room now. She has pneumonia."

"That's what I was concerned about. I think the facility waited too long to act on this, Dr. Bae."

"Well, let's get her admitted, and see how she does. How's Bob?"

"He's a bit weak, but since this is chemo week, and this is the second infusion with the new medication, I suspect it will get considerably worse."

"Hang in there, Jeanette." Dr. Bae is as concerned about me, the caregiver, as he is about Bob and Mom. "Let me know how it goes. You know you can call me any time." As I hang up the phone I wonder how so much compassion can fit in one person. I need to adopt this man. He would make a fine younger brother.

Keli and I re-strategize the day. She will drive Bob to his oncologist and then to his chemo infusion. This morning I need to focus on my mother. I will go straight to the hospital with her power of attorney for health care, along with documentation from Mom's attorney and physician stating as her decision-maker, I can overrule CPR and other lifesaving measures that could physically damage her delicate body.

I learned this lesson five years ago when an emergency room physician asked to see Mother's power of attorney for health care. I naively stated the document was, quite simply, a standard document. Yet, I had forgotten the news story that permeated our television sets for so long: the story about a young woman named Terry who had a massive heart attack, slipped into a coma, and suffered massive irreversible brain damage. It had been fifteen years since her collapse and her brain was half the size of a normal brain, but the feeding tubes locked her in a world between life and death or heaven and hell. Her husband wanted to let her go, but her parents challenged his decision in court.

I told the physician, "Mom's power of attorney is just a standard document," as I handed him the POA.

He looked at me and said, "Nothing is standard about these decisions. Not since the Terry Schiavo case. If your mother has a heart attack, we have to administer CPR unless you have the paperwork which states you are responsible for this decision, and you decide otherwise." I had to revisit Mother's attorney, have two physician's declare her incompetent, and have an addendum prepared to verify I could make these life and death decisions on her behalf. It was the only way to prevent medical professionals in an ambulance or an emergency room from beating on her failing heart while crushing her frail ribs into her lungs. There are no wins. We seek, instead, the least damage possible.

* * *

By the time I get to the hospital, my mother is lying in an ER cubicle with her chest heaving up and down, trying to get adequate air, but exhausted from lungs with too much infection, too much fluid. I wonder if this is it. Will she die today or will she try to hold on? Will this be the day I give my mother permission to let go? Permission to die? She must not worry about me, but I must prepare myself to let her go.

A sandy-haired physician walks in, crisp in his white coat, reading the history I have provided. He looks up from the chart, offers his hand and introduces himself. I tell him my name, extend my hand, then quickly retract it.

"I'm sorry, doctor. I shouldn't shake your hand. I have shingles. At first, I thought it was erythema nodosum, because it started at my elbow, red and swollen, but over the last few days it has evolved into a rash working down a nerve path from my elbow to my forearm, into the palm of my hand and finally my middle finger, so I have a case of shingles." My assessment is accurate, but I sound like a run-on sentence. Worse, I know the shingles virus can be contagious for those who have not had chicken pox. So I castigate myself for not having gloved coming into the emergency room, but I am too stressed to think about every damn detail, every damn issue, that keeps clouding my damn life.

"Are you a physician?" The doctor eyebrows arch as he looks at me, causing lines across his forehead.

I explain my knowledge does not come from medical school, but from necessity. I do not bore him with explanations about the medical research I do for sick friends, my own auto-immune diseases, or that I read college medical books for fun. He smiles and thanks me for not shaking his hand.

The doctor reviews Mother's x-ray results and blood work. His touch is light as he examines her. She looks so weak and listless and pale I fight my instincts to cradle her like a child. He shares his thoughts as they unfold, taking time to explain his conclusions.

"Your mother has pneumonia as well as some light emphysema in her right upper lobe."

Her pulmonologist and I spoke of this some months ago, so I explain to the doctor. "Yes, the emphysema is primarily related to the kyphosis in her spine." My mother's tiny frame tilts over and to the right side, compressing the right side of her lung. She is six inches shorter than she was fifteen years ago, but looks 25 years older. "How bad is the pneumonia?" I ask.

"The X-ray doesn't look that bad, but she is older so her immune system is weaker. She may have a difficult time overcoming this. We need to keep her here, and watch her for a few days."

"Thank you, Doctor. She needs a higher level of care than the facility can provide. She belongs in the hospital." We have a consensus. She will be taken upstairs to the fifth floor to be admitted. I like this man. I just can't remember his name. The fog in my brain is too thick.

As the doctor leaves, I reach for my purse to call Keli.

"How's Bob, Keli?"

"He's okay. He saw the oncologist, got his blood work so now we are at the infusion center. He is upstairs getting started. How's Elma?"

"Mom has pneumonia as Dr. Bae and I suspected. The X-ray confirmed it so they are admitting her now. She is too weak and too sick to go back to the facility."

"Jeanette, why don't I come across the street to the hospital and be with you and Elma while Bob has his infusion? It will take two hours for him to finish and I'm just sitting here. The nurses here at the infusion center have your number, don't they?" I can feel my lungs releasing air, no doubt air stale from being too tense to exhale fully for the last year of my life.

"Yeah, Keli, they do. They can call me if they have any concerns, or when Bob's infusion is done. It would be really nice to have you here for a while."

"Okay, I'll let Bob know and I'll be right there."

* * *

The hospital overlooks the bay surrounded by small islands engineered to create a boater's paradise, and it seems as if sparkling crystals float on blue ocean as boats rock gently on the quiet waters. Each morning the view from the waiting room on this floor is seductive. Each sunset the view is climactic. Mother has a private room without a view.

As I wait for the floor nurses to review their new patient, examining Mom from head to toe for any tears, abrasions, or bed sores, I mentally picture my week. Bob has chemo infusions every day this week, one more appointment with the oncologist, and possibly one or two transfusions to increase his red blood cells. Mother will be in the hospital at least four to five days judging by her current level of weakness. Wednesday is Bob's birthday. I know this will be his last; his white count is no longer controllable. We must create a memory, a celebration big enough to honor his life, yet small enough for his limited energy. Attendance will be limited to the three of us. If the next two days go as planned, I can plan a party. I think. *Really, Jeanette?* Perhaps, I should leave the celebration preparation to Keli.

* * *

I talk softly to Mother as she lies in her bed, monitors flashing graphs of heartbeats, blood pressure readings, and oxygen saturation levels while an IV tube hooked to bags of saline solution and antibiotics slowly drips into Mom's veins. The nebulizer mask covers her mouth and nose pumps air and medication into her lungs, lobes that by now are too weakened to draw in the level of oxygen required to protect her body and brain from harm.

A new doctor enters the room. He is a hospitalist, a physician who specializes in hospital care, one who takes over for the patient's primary care doctor once a patient has been admitted. The plan has its merits, but these physicians are disadvantaged by a lack of patient history, the very history residing in Dr. Bae's memory banks.

We introduce ourselves, yet his name slips away, too, like a wind-blown leaf. He walks me into the hall, explaining that patients, even very ill patients, can hear and often comprehend discussions about illness and even death. My insides drop like a steel crowbar as I wait to hear if this roller coaster is headed up or down.

He looks at me, white coat open covering tan slacks and a light blue shirt. He wears it well with his dark, almond eyes and black hair. He seems so young. Today, I feel so old.

"Mrs. Reese," the doctor draws a slow, deep breath. "Your mother is in a very weakened condition. You can hear the bronchitis throughout her bronchial tubes. As they told you in the emergency room, she has pneumonia. While it is fairly localized, it is dangerous for an older person. As we get older, our ability to fight infection wanes." He takes out a pen and starts to draw a graph on the back of a piece of paper he has in his hand. One line represents an infection in an older patient. The other line represents the decline in an elderly patient's immune system. Mom is at the dreaded intersect: the point where the infection becomes stronger than the immune response.

"At 84, your mother's body will have a fight to overcome this. I've ordered some strong antibiotics, oxygen, breathing treatments, but above and beyond that, it is up to her." I nod my head. He knows I get it.

"If she doesn't respond well to the antibiotics, it is time to consider hospice." *Time to consider hospice.* This phrase is different than the phrase delivered by Bob's oncologist last week, but the meaning is the same: we wait, we watch, we start hospice. It is all about "when." "Ifs" are not in doubt, only the "whens." *I hate "whens."*

Keli arrives and stands in the room beside Mother's bed. She picks up her hand and gently holds it in her own. She, too, has attached a piece of her heart to my mother. It is impossible to avoid. When Miss Elma, as Bob has come to call her, has any energy in her oh-so-little-self, she will greet you with a smile that could light the heavens, a heart that could warm the Arctic, and petite fingers that will take yours in hers while she plants her signature kiss on the back of your hand. It is Miss Elma's hug, Miss Elma's way of thanking people who help her. She could stamp the word "love" on your hand, but it would never convey the meaning as well as the lipstick left from "the kiss."

I summon Keli into the hall to update her on the doctor's assessment. She gets it. Keli herself has an inoperable brain tumor, or more likely remnants of one after the onslaught of chemo treatments. She has learned rich lessons in life, as she stares down fear by giving to others, and faces stress by smiling her broadest smile. She understands that while I cannot control the outcomes for my mother or my husband, I need to manage their care to ensure the quality of what little time they have left. Keli is a follower here—cooking, shopping, shuttling. Equally as important, she respects my lead.

I take a deep breath, and we both walk back into Mother's hospital room. The nurse attempts to replace the oxygen mask Mother routinely removes. Her eyes are closed much of the time, but she senses when no one is in the room and tugs on masks and tubes and paraphernalia that must seem unnatural and intrusive. The alarms go off, summoning nurses and aides. They return as needed, but hospitals are not staffed for one-on-one care. It helps I can calm Mother.

My phone rings and I recognize the warm, but steady voice of Vanessa, the chemo nurse. Bob's infusion is done. He is ready to be picked up. Keli strokes Miss Elma's arm, then heads out the door. She will find a restaurant that serves food Southern enough to entice Bob to eat, most likely scrambled eggs with bacon and sausage and grits, comfort food high in fat, but able to satisfy his Southern taste buds. Besides, heart disease is not the concern at this point.

I cannot join them for lunch, but I have comfort knowing for today Bob is stable. Instead, I focus on how to ensure someone is here with Mother, someone who can sooth her as she struggles with tubes and masks—be it day or night. Today, her needs are complex like a rolling desert sandstorm waiting to unleash. By the end of the week it could be Bob's sandstorm, but my thoughts cannot travel that far into the future.

Survival does not allow it.

The Permission Speech
January 2011

Mom was beautiful, and at 84-years-old, she still brings light into a room when she can smile. She reared four children, sold real estate, helped my father run a business, and somehow found the energy—in the quiet of the night—to dance saucy little dances for my father before retiring to bed.

As I watch her now, her chest works to pull the air into her lungs, shoulders heaving up and down in rhythm. Her pulse is 96, normal for her now. Yesterday it was too low. The day before it jumped to 145 as her frail heart poured its energy into keeping her alive. I know she does not have much time left. I know it can be helpful to give a patient permission to die, *but how do I have that conversation with my own mother?*

"How are you doing, Mom?"

I lean over to kiss her. Her eyes meet mine, and her nose wrinkles a bit. She would love to tell me how she is doing. She would love to ask me how I am doing, but the muscles that jerk her limbs also freeze her face until her smile becomes a grimace, and her words are stuck inside her mind. She has learned to wrinkle her nose to let me know she is there when she cannot speak.

When the freezing subsides and she does speak, she fights with her words as if they are pieces of a puzzle tossed too high in the air, and scatter on the floor in a way that makes no sense. Mom shakes her head with sadness as she hears the confused mix coming from her own lips.

I used to ask, "What came out of your mouth wasn't what you were thinking, was it?" Her chest would deflate as she would lower her head and gently shake it side to side.

Each time I saw this sadness, my heart wanted to crawl into a hole and die for her.

For the past thirteen years, Mother's Parkinson's and dementia have overwhelmed her once-vibrant, intelligent self. It is hard to watch her decline as each day steals more of her from me, taking pieces of my heart right out of my chest. Each day I pick those pieces up and place them back in my heart. Then, I look for my smile to put it back on my face.

As she lies in the hospital fighting with frozen muscles and a congested heart, she tries to nod "yes" when I ask if she is okay. She does not want to worry the daughter who has become the mother. Sometimes I want to hold her. Sometimes I want to curl up in God's lap and hide.

Too much worry takes energy, leaving me wanting to snap something—anything—in two. So, I search for a laugh, a funny story to find my smile. I get this from my mother. She had a way of gifting her humor, sometimes unintentionally, as she did during a hospital stay a couple of years ago.

* * *

Lying in the hospital bed, Mother was listless, limp-limbed, and her eyes were closed for hours. I was so sure it was her time to go, I picked up her hand, gently holding it in mine, and gave her the "speech": permission to die.

"Mom, you know how much I love you, and I will miss you so much when you are gone, but if you want to go be with Dad and your mother and father, I understand."

The corner of her right eye began to open, then the other eye opened until both eyes were open just wide enough to give me a glance, then she turned her face toward the wall.

"I love you, and I will miss you so much, but I do understand." My heart ached at the thought of her passing.

She gave me one more glance, then pointed her delicate finger to the TV balancing on the wall, and said with firmness in her voice, "I want to watch that!"

"You what?"

"I want to watch THAT!" She pointed again at the television. The word "television" escaped her mind, but her sentence was complete—a rare treat for me, and no doubt for Mother.

"Sure, Mom, let me turn it on for you."

"And I want to have Christmas."

It was the end of October. Christmas was eight weeks off.

"Oh, you would like to have Christmas early?" *I get it. She doesn't want to miss Christmas.* "Sure, Mom, we can have it early."

"No, I want Christmas *at* Christmas." She continued to look at the TV. She was clearly done talking with me. She was not mad, just done with the subject. I understand the need for the "permission speech." I have read about it, and heard people discuss it. I can understand how helpful it might be for a loved one to have the conversation, but how the hell does one know WHEN to give permission to a patient to die? I may never know when to have this conversation with her, but it will not be anywhere close to a television set.

It was the speech that went nowhere. I'm still unclear about giving someone permission to die, but I do know this: Mother would not want me to lose myself in the process of her dying. She would tell me she loves me, life goes on—and then she would tell me to go turn on the TV.

Leftovers
February 2011

Bob is a pistol today. He sits in his easy chair, feet propped up on the coffee table, but his forehead is tense and his eyes could spit fire. It is chemo week again, a week of daily infusions. This is day four: the fourth day of his transformation into what appears to be a state of semi-controlled rage.

"I'm hungry," he barks, "Let's go get something to eat."

"Honey, I'm so tired. Let's just eat leftovers." Between caring for Bob, visiting my mother at the facility or the hospital, and managing my own chronic pain, driving to the curb would be too much tonight.

"I don't want leftovers." As his chest rises, I can hear the resolve in his words.

"Bob," my voice sounds like an irritated mother running low on patience, "what is wrong with leftovers?"

His lips purse and his eyes glare at me like steely white laser lights. "I am *not* going to eat leftovers!" He is not fond of my cooking. Right now he is not fond of me.

"Bob, I'm tired. I don't want to go out again tonight. Besides it is 95 degrees outside."

"Fine, I'll go myself." I know this is not a good idea. Last month, he backed my car into the car of an elderly gentleman. That bumper was replaced. A few days later he drove my new bumper into a wall. This month, he parked his car at the grocery store, and managed to rip off his entire front bumper. He did not call our emergency towing service. He decided to drive the car home, pushing the barely connected bumper in front of his auto at five miles per hour. He was more than two miles from home.

His car is being repaired. My car is the only car in the garage, and it sits like a waiting duck with its neck tucked in, hiding under its wings.

"You'll go to dinner by yourself?"

"Yes. I'll go alone."

His petulance is perfect, and it is pissing me off. "In what car?"

"Are you saying you don't want me to drive your car?" He got that right. Bob is not a friendly driver on non-chemo weeks, but on chemo weeks I question his judgment, not just his temperament.

"Bob, how many bumpers have we gone through lately?" My tone sets him off.

"Fine, just fine! I'll walk to a restaurant!" He is standing now, stomping a bit as well.

"Bob, you can't walk outside in this heat. Besides, you would be walking on a four lane road with no sidewalks." At the moment, I cannot seem to show my concern, but my irritation is as thick as a cloud. I am not pretty.

"Well, I'm going anyway." He storms to the door and walks out—no water, no cell phone, just attitude.

He'll be back. But he does not walk back in the door. After a few minutes, I call his always-down-to-earth sister and tell her about my snapping turtle comments, Bob's stubborn temper: the whole story. We both chuckle under our breath, but she can tell I am concerned.

She tells me what I already know, but still need to hear. "Well, Jeanette, I reckon you need to get in the car and go look for him. That's what I'd do." Her simple words resonate with wisdom—the wisdom of distance from the glaring contest of two entrenched wills.

I grab the car keys from my purse, and drive down the hill looking for my husband, a man with a ball of white cotton taped over a vein on his left arm. I remember the little pizza place, turn into the strip mall, and park outside its front door. He is inside ordering a sandwich. Watching him stand at the counter, I can breathe more comfortably, and my heart beats more slowly. He walks out the door, planning on hiking back up the steep hill to our home.

I roll down my window to make him an offer. "Hey, you want a ride?"

Bob turns his head toward the car. His movements are slow and it is as if I can see the fatigue overtaking each cell in his body. He gives me a half-hearted stubborn look, but his edginess wanes as the exhaustion gains on his chemically controlled emotions.

"I guess so." He nods his head, opens the door, and climbs in the car. I hand him a bottle of cold water. He unscrews the lid and begins to drink.

I put my hand on his arm. "Let's go home." His shoulders drop as though a hint of relief has passed through his muscles. I turn and look at him, thankful he is safe. I do not know why this chemo changes this man I love. I do not know how much longer I will have him. The only thing I know for certain is that I will be the one to drive us both home.

Tornados
February 2011

*I hope you see, feel, accept, believe,
and want my commitment to a life-long
relationship of love with you. 'Tis true.*
Robert Canady, May 17, 1995

Today's oncology appointment is standard, if not habitually tedious as the doctor palpates Bob's abdomen, listens to his clear lungs, and the sounds of his pumping heart. I am hopeful about our visit today. Bob's physician will be starting him on a new chemo. During our first office visit eight months ago, Dr. Miller expressed confidence when he said Bob could have five to six years left. The doctor's comment had eased some of my fear, yet as I watched my husband's quick decline, a different timeline rattled through my thoughts, a shorter one, maybe one or two years. The thought brewed at the back of my consciousness like a tornado building across a great landscape.

He is ready for our questions now. The first one comes from me.

"Dr. Miller, if this chemotherapy doesn't lower Bob's white count, what's next?" I want to be ready to research it on the Internet.

The doctor listens to me, then switches his gaze to my husband, one set of blue eyes fixed on the other.

"Well, Bob," he pauses for second or two. "If this chemo doesn't work, it means the cancer cells have become immune to the chemo."

His comment startles me. *Cancer cells can outsmart chemo?* I imagine the cancer cells simply ignoring the harsh chemicals being pumped into Bob's veins. Then I realize the same is true with bacteria and antibiotics. Many chemos *will* knock out existing cancer cells, but some cancer cells are tough, and they mutate in ways that protect them from the chemo. So these mutated cells grow, reproduce, and spread, but because they are immune, they do not die. Cancer cells are so smart they can live on until the host gives out. I shudder realizing my husband is the host.

The doctor continued. "That's why the first chemo didn't slow the leukemic blasts. The cancer cells became immune." The doctor focuses on Bob's face, and selects his next words carefully as though laying a wreath upon a grave. "Our next step would be to make you comfortable."

Make Bob comfortable? Comfortable? My heart rate quickens inside my chest, my brain is on fire, but my face holds steady. I want to be angry with the doctor, but I can't. I want to be so angry I could shove his honest words right back in his mouth, but I can't. I know Bob has an expiration date. I know I will lose him at some point, but today I wanted to hear a list of follow-up chemos waiting in line capable of killing a million leukemia cells a minute forcing a fast and furious check-mate to buy my husband more time. That is what we expected with the first chemo. *How can cancer cells be so fucking smart?*

We get in the car and drive home, saying little about doctors, nurses or leukemia. It is as if we did not hear what the doctor said, but we did. It is as though a diagnosis of leukemia changes nothing, but it does. It is as if he is not going to die, but he will.

As we drive down the freeway, the cancer cells dance in my husband's body while a tornado is silently building across the sky of my mind.

Last Birthday
March 2011

It is Wednesday, the 9th of March. If I died today, it would be the result of a life too full. Mother is in the hospital facing hospice. Bob is having another round of chemo. And today is his birthday—his 81st. My heart tells me it will be the last birthday I have with him.

It is a two-car day again. Keli drives to the hospital to see Mother. I drive Bob to his doctor's appointment. I am so pleased he is starting a new chemo today, chemo number three with yet another name I have not yet mastered. The first two chemos did not stop nor slow the leukemic blasts, the raw unformed white blood cells have taken over my husband's blood.

I drive Bob to his infusion, drop him with the oncology nurses, then drive to the hospital to help with Mother. The nurses in charge of my mother's case take me aside. When they step out of Mother's room, they tell me, she tears the mask off her face and pulls the IV from her arm, causing her O2 levels to dive. They can't do it alone. She needs a caregiver, they say.

Ruth, one of Mother's caregivers from the year before, takes the 12-hour night shift for the remainder of the week. Then, she drives to her part-time day job. For the last two days, I have managed the care during the 12-hour day shift, but it steals what little time I have left with Bob. Yesterday, I called a brother asking if he might drive across two counties to sit with Mom today. His car was not in good enough shape. I told him I would rent him a car, that I just want to spend Bob's last birthday with him. Perhaps it was his mood, but it angered him. He hung up. I realize I do not have the luxury of devoting time to the long standing dysfunction of our family. There is nothing to be gained at this point. Like a rolling sand storm in a vast desert, the thick dust lands on everyone and chokes the love out of the family. Out of necessity, I move on.

While I sit with Mother, Keli takes Bob home after his infusion. Exhausted from the chemo, he lies on the couch, and once his eyelids close he slips into a slumber so deep, the living world evaporates from his mind. Keli, intent on creating a birthday celebration, slips down to the store. She is a slender woman, about seven years younger than me, an inch or two shorter than me, and perhaps an inch or two wider. She is lovely, and men watch her. One day, an older gentleman asked me if she was my daughter. Wrong question, I told him, but to this day I still laugh about it. She is ageless in her standard red turtleneck sweater and jeans. No, she is not my daughter, but she has become my sister.

At the store, she purchases anything that might be festive enough to create a celebration, then carefully hides it from Bob's view. Bob, still in a deep sleep, never realized she had slipped out.

When 7:30 arrives, Mother tired from another day of pneumonia, falls asleep, and for the moment, the masks and IV are safe from her small hands. Her caregiver will be arriving at the hospital soon, so I quietly trek to the garage and start the 30-mile drive home. My body is weary, too, but I am anxious to get home to see my husband.

When I walk in the house, Bob is still fast asleep on the couch with his USC snuggly blanket draped over his body. It was a gag gift from friends at his 80th birthday party. Initially, he wore it with an alma mater confidence, his strong chest popping with pride. The first night it was given to him, he brought it home, lay down on the couch, USC letters adorning his frame, and promptly took a quick nap.

Now, he wraps it around his whole body trying to stay warm and alive.

I move quietly up the stairs to the shower. I glance in the mirror and notice a 59-year-old woman who looks tired, one who knows she must find the energy for her husband. First, a day in the hospital requires removal of all bacteria that may have climbed onto my frame. My clothing is dumped in the dirty clothes hamper, and I step under the warm water. I refuse to put Bob at risk. By 8:30, I am clean enough to hug my husband, and have a short birthday celebration.

The kitchen has become the hub of our home, like a warm room in a little cottage carefully infused with memories. The front of the fridge is covered with pictures, all of people we love, some alive, some not, but each photograph is a snapshot of life passing by. Bob is still sleeping under his snuggly on the couch. Keli stands at one of the kitchen counters, now so covered with birthday decorations the granite countertop barely shows through. There *will* be a party for Bob. Keli has created it. We three will celebrate one last birthday of Bob's life. She is truly an amazing friend.

Bob's cousin, Kim, sent a fruit arrangement that arrived earlier today with a birthday greeting. So festive, it resembles a floral display, with wooden sticks for stems, and colorful fruit cut in wonderful shapes at the end of each stem. The green melon is cut in quarter moons, the yellow pineapple in stars, and the strawberries and bananas are dipped in chocolate.

Keli quietly prepares the table. She pulls the coconut cream pie, Bob's favorite, out of the fridge and sets it on the tabletop. The ten candles, no doubt the number we happened to have in the cupboard, are green and yellow and sparingly positioned around the pie. The tan placemats with green napkins are already in place. They are not a festive color, but they are clean. She bought Bob a bouquet of carnations and multi-colored balloons that reach for the ceiling while tethered to their colorful strings. When we wake Bob, she wants the party in play.

I lean over and kiss my husband. It brings him out of his slumber, and he smiles. "You're home," he says quietly, tired eyes looking up at me.

"Babe," I touch his arm, and continue. "We have a surprise for you! Look what Keli has done."

He sits ups and looks toward the table and his expression turns to one of wonder much like a child. He rarely, if ever, expects people to do special things for him. While obvious to those of us around him, he fails to realize how exceptional he is.

We take pictures of the table with all its flowers, and fruit and pie. Then Keli takes a picture of Bob and me, my arms around his waist, smiling into his face, while his head is tilted toward me as he looks into the camera. I know it will be one of the last pictures of us together. My smile is just for him. Five years from now when I look at this picture, I will still feel that love.

He is like a kid around coconut cream pie. He cuts the pie, dishes it out, smearing whipped cream here and there, then sticks his thumb in his mouth to lick it clean grinning like a five-year-old who has found a treasure. His grin always unraveled me in a way hard to explain. I have always used layers of armor to keep men away. Once I knew Bob, one grin, one teasing comment, and all that protection vanished. Unlike other men, he went straight to my heart. I am so safe with him. I want him alive so much, there are times I cannot allow the word "die" to pass my lips. I am not afraid of being alone. I just love this person, this man, my lover, but fate is not our friend.

The Cell From Hell
April 2011

My phone does not work. It makes me want to spit fire, my nostrils flare, and find something, anything other than my hard plastic phone, upon which to gnash my teeth. How is it that this week, the week when Mother is critical, the week when Bob has crucial chemo infusions, is the week the Devil seems to have taken control of my phone? My personal fuse is shorter than the length of an ant's body, and the Devil does not stand a chance. Under my breath, I curse the three letters of my cell phone company. One at a time.

As I drive into the shopping center, I spot the AT&T logo, pull into a parking space directly in front of the door while curbing my desire to run my car over the sidewalk plunging it into the large glass door. Surely my control is a true testament I am a peaceful, nonviolent woman.

I walk in the door to find a nice young man standing behind the counter.

"Hi, I need some help." He looks up at me, wearing a smile.

"What can I do for you?"

"Well, my cell is acting really strange."

"I'm sorry, Ma'am, but you will have to call AT&T to report a malfunctioning phone."

"Here's the deal. My mother is in the hospital, and the nursing staff couldn't get through on my phone. My husband is having chemo this week, and the nurses couldn't reach me. It is critical I have a reliable phone, and this one is clearly not reliable. I don't have the time to deal with AT&T on the phone. I need you to take care of this for me."

He looks at me and ditches his allegiance to company policy.

"Sure. Be happy to help."

AT&T phone support messes with him for forty-five minutes, wasting his time, badgering him, doing what they can to prevent him from getting me a replacement phone. I watch as he painstakingly outmaneuvers them, finally convincing them to overnight me a new cell. I could have managed the devil, but I would have been chopped liver for AT&T phone support. I thank him, and I thank him again.

The cell arrives the next day. It, too, is defective. While Bob's veins are filling with chemo, Keli stays with Mom in the hospital, and I drive back to the cell phone store. I pull up hoping the same young man will be waiting for me, as if his own phone antennae could pick up my telepathic SOS message. I push the large plate glass doors open once again. He is nowhere in sight, but I am grateful there is no line, no large contingent of customers cornering the two sales staff on the floor. I do not want to compete with customers wanting to purchase new phones with fat contracts of five thousand minutes a month. With no customers in the store, helping me has to be more interesting than dusting product. Besides, I am a stressed woman with a goal and very little time.

"Hi, I need some help." The young man looks up from his own phone.

"Okay, how can I help you?"

I explain about the old cell, the new cell, the urgency to have a functional cell, my mother, my husband, but he just looks at me waiting for the right moment to interrupt.

"I'm sorry. You'll have to call AT&T." I feel my neck getting warm. Poor kid. He doesn't realize how hard a woman can fight when she has a mother and a husband facing hospice.

"I'd really like you to make the call for me. They are really difficult on the phone, and I really don't have the time." I can feel I am far too eager to put on the gloves.

"I'm sorry. You'll have to call AT&T yourself." *What part of customer service does AT&T not understand?* I study this young man for a split second, about a split second longer than I care to, and I notice he is several inches taller than the young man who assisted me two days ago. It appears his IQ is several points lower.

"I really need you to do this." I steady myself.

"Ma'am, you will have to call AT&T yourself." Now my head and my neck are getting warmer, but his head is still attached to his neck, so I figure I have not lost enough control—yet. I lean over the counter, and peer at his name tag.

"Mark," my face gets closer to his so he can see into my steely blue eyes, perhaps feel the heat starting to steam off my shoulders. "Don't even MESS with me! I am NOT in the mood. Get on the phone and call customer service. Now!"

He looks at me as if his mother just whacked him upside the head.

"Yes, Ma'am." He picks up the phone, his insolence fades into timidity and he dials—feverishly. I step back from the counter, and take a deep, satisfying breath with sure confidence I will get another replacement phone.

When he finishes the call, I thank him. I don't tell him he is lucky his head still sits on his shoulders. It would not be nice, but I do notice a certain sense of accomplishment.

It might be stress. It might be age. But I believe I have achieved Bitchdom. I think I just might like this.

Quiet Conversations
May 2011

I made reservations to visit my
daughter, Candy, to attend my
granddaughter's graduation. My
daughter, Karen, and her son will be
driving to join us.
It will be wonderful to see them.

Robert Canady, May 14, 1995

He is going to die. I can feel it. He is the one with cancer coming out of his bones, but it is as though I can feel it in mine. My husband will die one of the two ways leukemia patients die. He will bleed to death because his blood is slowly losing its ability to clot. Or, he will develop an infection, because his white cells can no longer fight off inbound viruses and bacteria. The white cells *are* the cancer now. They have been transformed and they roam his body like useless pieces of debris, like drunken guards outside a prison wall, instead of operating like the first line of defense.

During his calls across the country with his children and his sisters, he gives them partial information, and avoids the tough talks that require such terminal honesty, discussions that can only cause sadness. But his children and sisters deserve to know the truth. It is the right thing to do. So, I decide I will call his children one by one, testing gently for permission to tell them the whole story, the whole truth, about their father's illness.

Yet there are risks.

I choose my words carefully, deliberately, as though tiptoeing through a field with explosives hidden under its dirt. It is a situation of competing needs. Bob needs his children and his sisters. They need him. But they all live across the continent: from DC to Kansas to Georgia to Florida. Each airline flight in is a flying basket of germs. Each hug, each greeting, is another vehicle for the one last infection to take hold of my husband's body. Yes, this is a time of competing needs. There are hearts that must be brought together before this difficult loss, and there is a seriously ill patient that has the right to be protected from dying sooner than necessary. Yes, there are risks.

I could follow Bob's lead with his children and his sisters, letting them believe all is calm, that the treatment seems to be going fine. After all, theirs is a family culture of things left unsaid, topics understood to be off-limits. It confuses me, having come from a family where everything was said, be it anger or joy, embarrassing or not. I had to learn boundaries, but the unwritten rules of Bob's family feel like the same field of mines to me, and I never really know where my foot must be placed. Bob dances around the facts, perhaps because he does not want to face death, but more likely because he wants to protect the ones around him he loves so deeply: his children, his sisters, and me.

Yet following his lead seems wrong, just wrong. Every part of me knows his family would want to see him one last time, have one last conversation, have one last hug before he dies. I must speak the truth before the opportunity is gone. And so, I pick up my phone.

"I am not sure how much your father has told you about his condition. If there is additional information about your father's illness, would you want to know?" I approach his children with the tenderness they deserve.

"Yes. Yes, I would." The response is the same with each of his children, so we compare notes on what he has shared with them, and what the doctor has told us. They each understand. There is not much time left to visit, so his daughter moves her visit up several weeks. His oldest son schedules a visit. His youngest son, in between jobs, has already come to help two times and stays on alert in case we need his assistance again.

As Bob moves toward death, I know it is a path I cannot stop. God's hands are larger than mine and I do not own this process, but like a shepherd managing its flock, I am intent on doing what I can to protect my husband. If Bob's children fly in during chemo weeks, a time when his immune response is at its lowest, I hand each one a wash cloth and a towel as they step into the bathroom to rid themselves of the pesky bacteria collected on the flight. When a close friend flies in from Canada and becomes ill on the third day of his visit, he departs quickly, and I wash his sheets, then disinfect the guest bathroom, the refrigerator door, and any other handle he may have touched. Visits to my own hospitalized mother, result in complete showers before greeting my husband with a hug. It is not known whether this will give him the immense amount of protection he needs, but we all try. No, I cannot stop death, but I will do everything I can to prevent death from stealing my husband any sooner than it must.

When the kids come, I make sure I leave for several hours, allowing them father and child time alone, time to complete the relationships that, like many father/child bonds, have been taut with angst here and there through the years. But this is a time of forgiving, of sharing all the love in one's heart. Karen helps her father plan his service, a candid conversation, and one he had not been able to have until she arrived. He is so grateful.

His oldest son arrives, and while I know less about the conversations between them, Bob is so pleased. As they embrace for the last time, standing on the sidewalk outside the airport terminal, Bob tells him, "See you in the next life, Son." Bob smiles recounting his story, yet the tears brim in his eyes.

I call his sisters, too, as the bonds in their nuclear family were formed by the loss of their father, their farm, and the emotional upheaval of World War II. When asked, one sister encourages me to share any additional medical information I might know about her brother, and so I do. She understands the implications.

His other sister responds differently, but not unlike a person pained by the impending loss of someone close. "No. I don't need more information." Her words are clipped. "My brother has told me everything." I am saddened for I have heard what her brother has shared with her. He has kept much to himself. She may not have the facts, but she has a right to *not* know, too. My job is to support this process, but to do so, I must be in step with her reality, and so I tell her I am happy she feels she has what she needs. In the end, nothing else is of much concern. There is no reason to cause her pain.

He is saddened his sisters do not come, as am I, yet we know fewer people means less exposure to infections capable of ending his life early. Besides, as in many families, the mending in life is between parents and children, and it is the same in Bob's life. The right people visit, and during these times, we find the process of dying is beyond doctors, chemo and blood transfusions. It slips into the heart, into the letting go of old hurts, into the talk of love that must be acknowledged, and into saying goodbye. He does it all with each family member who comes to visit. And he does it so well. I am pleased for him.

We are lucky. In spite of the flight across country, in spite of the flu season, Bob does not become ill. And so we march on with chemo visits, hospitalizations, and infusions while I visit Mother in the facility or the hospital, depending on her condition. She is on hospice now. I go where I am needed, knowing eventually I will be exposed to some disease floating around the hospital or the facility. It seems most everything I do could put Bob in danger.

On Sunday, one of Mother's friends at the facility stands behind me and coughs over my shoulder. She is sick and the fear I feel drains my body. On Monday, a man sitting in the physician's waiting room, coughs before he covers his mouth. I look up to observe the man, wondering if he has something contagious, but he is some feet away from both Bob and me. I am exhausted watching, calculating, fearful of others, but still feel as tough as a mother bear.

Tuesday night, I go to bed with my husband. On Wednesday, I awaken feeling odd. Not sick, just odd, but it is enough to seek out Bob's physician.

"Just stay away from him, Jeanette. He has no immunity."

By nightfall there are still no definable symptoms, yet I move out of our bedroom, just in case, and sleep in the hall on the floor. I want to be close if he calls out, but I wear a mask and gloves when I come near him. The next day I fall asleep feeling fine, yet awaken Friday at 6:00 AM with what feels like a weight on my chest. The symptoms are severe enough to suggest the flu rather than a simple cold, and it invades my lungs with a deep congestion. There is no doubt I am very contagious now.

I reach Dr. Bae at 8:00 AM, and he calls in a prescription for strong antibiotics knowing he needs to treat me swiftly with a two-fisted punch, so he can protect Bob and my mother. With Crohn's Disease, it will take months, if not years, for my colon to recover from these strong antibiotics, but it no longer matters.

By Saturday morning, I am too sick to help Bob. He is too weak to help himself, so I call his son. It is 8:00 AM California time, 11:00 AM Florida time.

"Hey Ron, when are you scheduling your next trip to see your Dad?"

"I'm planning to be there in about three weeks. Why?"

"Well, I woke up sick yesterday morning, and I'm afraid to be near Bob, but he isn't strong enough to take care of himself. Is it possible for you to come sooner?"

"Jeanette, give me a few minutes and I'll call you back." He calls back in thirty minutes. "I'll be landing at the airport at 10:30 tonight, and will be at the house by 11:15." I am stunned, relieved, and amazed. I would be honored to wash Ron's feet upon his arrival were I not sick.

That night, Bob turns off the television, moves from the family room to the living room, and sits in a chair with a view of the street. He crosses his legs and sets his hands on the arms of the large, black chair and calmly waits until his son arrives. Ron arrives right on time; a habit he must have inherited from his father. Bob grins at the sight of his son getting out of the cab. Ron bounces in the door, smiling, with his hand out in need of cab fare. He barely had time to pack, let alone stop at a bank. I suspect he is starving, but all is well. The smile on Ron's face is perfect for Bob's soul.

I move from sleeping in the hall to sleeping in my workout room. Ron has the guest bedroom, and Bob stays in our master suite. I hate not sleeping with Bob. I want to watch him while he sleeps—just a few more times before I lose him. I want to be able to reach over and touch his muscular arms, the hair on his chest, but I can't. By the next morning, Bob awakens, comes out of the bedroom, his face tight with fear. He is trying to fill his lungs with air.

The doctor on call has his opinion. "He needs antibiotics, Jeanette."

My God, *I know that!* I wonder why I even called, because it does not matter what the doctor says, at this point. I know Bob belongs in the hospital, so the three of us pile in the car.

While he coughs and hacks, the emergency room physician examines Bob, then makes the decision to admit him to the hospital. The doctor wears his concern on his face. I wear a mask, gloves and a paper gown, yet keep my distance and sit across the sterile room. I take a picture of my husband lying on the gurney, draped in his white gown, for reasons I do not fully understand, but my heart tells me I must have something to hold, something representing the man I love, the man I cannot touch.

As I sit there, it becomes clear the odds are not in Bob's favor, that he may not survive this infection. He survived the chemo. He made it through all the visits from his family, all the visits from his friends. He made it through everyone—except me—the one who tried to protect him from everything.

May 18, 2011

My Love,

It was so wonderful this morning to be able to tell you how much I miss and love you, and ... to hear it from you. It thrilled me to no end. I simply wandered about my office in a daze. Knowing you were there was so comforting and loving for me. It was almost more than I could do to not blurt out "She called me!!!"

Robert Canady, May 18, 1995

Bob looks at me with a slightly goofy look, as though he is trying to tell me something. The bed is elevated at a 45-degree angle as he rests his head against his pillows, and his hospital-white gown covers his shoulders and chest. Bob is not goofy. While he seems comfortable under the white sheet and thin blanket draped over his six-foot muscular frame, something is not quite right, and I cannot make sense of what I see.

His son had the night shift last night, sleeping on a cot next to his father's bed. The day shift is mine, but we are both with him during the evening. When one of us is at Bob's side, the other is at a hotel down the street from the hospital, resting, preparing for our next shift. We do not want him to be alone, as much for ourselves as for Bob, so we hold on to each day, each hour we have left with him. When I drove his son back to the hotel this morning, he told me his dad was acting funny. "He's looped on those pain drugs."

Bob's head sways as he tries to focus on me. The evening before, he had made a request. "Babe, would you clean my glasses?" I steamed them with my breath, polished them with my sweater. I handed him his glasses, and he settled them on the bridge of his nose and over his ears. My husband turned to look into my face. It was then his expression changed and his shoulders slumped.

"Oh," he paused as his glance cast downward. "It's not my glasses. It's my left eye. I can see all around you, but I can't see your face. The center of my vision is black." He removed his glasses, clutching them as he lowered his hand to his side. "My right eye is starting to have black spots, too." I knew immediately he had developed a retinal bleed—in each eye.

It occurred to me how much we express love through our eyes, our smiles. He would not see mine anymore. It must have been so hard for him. For me, it was as though a shield had been erected between us, forcing us to face the first step of saying goodbye.

* * *

Today, when Bob tries to talk, it is as though the world around him is a bit senseless, definitely confusing to him. He tries to tell me something, to put words together, yet his words do not seem to be in his control. I have never seen him like this before.

"I want to be in the chapel," he tells me. I assume he is confirming what he has told me before: he does not want his service in the church, but in the funeral home chapel. I assure him I have already shared this information with his family in Georgia.

"I want you to sit on the judge's lap." What is he trying to tell me? We do not even know a judge. I touch his arm and declare with softness in my voice I have no desire to sit on anyone's lap but his. *Is his thinking impaired, or is it his ability to verbalize his thoughts?* I cannot tell. So, I start to guess at the meaning behind his words. *Is he is telling me when he is gone, I must move on?* Hell would ice over before I could be ready for that.

As I watch my husband's disorientation, I wonder if the doctor has seen Bob today. He is expected to be discharged tomorrow, his pneumonia seemingly under control. But his white count is high, a result of cancerous white blood cells reproducing wildly as they morph into leukemic blasts. His platelet count is too low, leaving his blood virtually unable to clot. The hospital staff gives him transfusions daily now. Yet, traces of Bob's blood seep through different orifices as though tempting death. Such is the course of acute leukemia. It skillfully plays a seductive melody like a phantom piper until all the cells, both red and white, hear the deadly tune and march off a cliff in unison.

Bob's breakfast still sits on the tray. Although confused, he seems amenable to eating so I spoon small amounts into his mouth watching as he chews and swallows. Suddenly, food begins to come back up, not with force. It simply emerges from behind closed lips. I help him clear his mouth, then pick up his medical chart and begin to search for clues. *Something is not right.*

Perhaps his son is correct. He is on four different narcotics to control undiagnosed pain in his abdomen and hip, but why so many? Even for a 200-pound male, four narcotics seem like a dangerous overkill. I take the red call button in my hand and press it. I want the nurse in here. Now.

She has been the nurse on Bob's case since the morning shift change. Long, dark hair clamped tightly to her head, she is pleasant looking in a rounded way. She is also confused by Bob's behaviors, so she starts checking his vitals. "You've got him on four narcotics. Don't you think that is too much? He's vomiting. What if the medications are making him sick?"

She looks at me and says, "He's only on three meds, Mrs. Reese."

"No, he is on four. It's in the chart."

The nurse counts the meds that have been added over the last three days and realizes I am right. She starts making calls, leaves and comes back with a syringe in hand of yet another medication. This time it is an anti-narcotic, a med that will erase the effects of the four drugs floating in his system. By now, Bob's body is overly mobile, if not loose, appearing as if he has had several shots of whiskey. These movements are strange to observe in a man who rarely drinks more than one beer at a time.

My phone rings. It is a close friend calling for an update. There is a waiting room down the hall, so I take the call, and leave the nurse standing at Bob's side preparing to inject the medication into his IV drip. Another friend calls, then I make a call, and time runs by as though each minute is in a marathon. I begin to feel concerned, even have feelings of guilt, because I am not in the room with my husband.

When I walk to his door, I find four nurses standing in Bob's room. No one is smiling. My husband is clearly uncomfortable. Alarmed I comment, "What? I leave for a few minutes and now there is a party going on? What happened?" The nurses turn and look at me, and the head nurse begins to speak.

"We aren't sure yet. We are taking your husband to x-ray for a CAT scan. We'll know more once we see the results."

"What happened when you gave him the anti-narcotic?"

"We're not sure. That's why we need a CAT scan."

I know what happened. Once the drug was in his system, the nurse observed something—something that concerned her. A few hours ago, there was conversation about taking Bob home tomorrow. Now, he is having a STAT CAT scan.

Bob, his IV, and his bed are pushed out the door by two nurses, one on each side as they head to the Radiology Department. The third nurse walks out of the room, and heads down the hall in the opposite direction. The nurse assigned to his case stays with me. She is too smart to assure me with false promises of healing, but she gives me no hints, no leads on what might be happening to my husband. I thank her, she leaves, and I pick up my phone.

"Ron, something's wrong with your dad." My words are clipped and fast. "They just rushed him downstairs for a CAT scan. I need to swing by and pick you up at the hotel, and get you back here while they are doing the scan. I want to be in Bob's room when he gets back."

By the time we return, Bob is being wheeled back into his hospital room. He is sedated now, more comfortable and I feel the tension in my body begin to release. His regular nurse comes to the room to tell me I have a phone call at the nurse's station. "The physician on Bob's case wants to speak to you." I follow the nurse to the phone, grateful I will finally hear the results of the CAT scan.

The black phone sits on a counter in front of the nurse's station, where two nurses sit at the desk, and three others talk as they stand at the station. They grow quiet as I walk toward them. There is no privacy here. Bob's nurse glides to the other side. As I lift the receiver to my ear, she leans toward me and whispers, "I'm so sorry." The doctor had not had a chance to say a word. He didn't need to.

"Mrs. Reese, your husband has had a significant bleed in his brain. His platelet count is so low, his blood isn't clotting well. This happens with leukemia. I don't know what your wishes are, but I can have a neurosurgeon there as soon as possible."

"You will *not* call in a neurosurgeon to operate on a dying man. I will not let anyone put him through more. It is simply not fair, and it's not what he would want. You will let him die in peace."

"I agree with your decision, Mrs. Reese. We will make him as comfortable as possible." I thank her, set the phone down on its cradle, and stare at some small item sitting on the counter. I do not even know what the item is. I just stand there with an odd sense of staring at it. It is as though a thick cloud has surrounded the nurse's station, a haze so thick that for the moment, it seems to control my thoughts.

I was going to take my husband home tomorrow. I will be driving home without him. The rhythm of my heart has changed.

Suddenly, Bob's nurse is at my side, her arms wrapping around me, and she again says, "I'm so sorry." I let her embrace me, but I do not have a sense if I am responding. All I know is my husband is dying. And he is dying now. I walk back to Bob's room. I must tell Ron, who sits at his father's side, holding his hand. I touch my husband's shoulder, and look up at his son.

This won't be easy.

I see the nurses attaching Bob's monitors to the hospital bed, but the fog in my mind is too thick, so their fast movements seem a blur in my visual field. They are preparing to move him to ICU, a place where patients are transferred to keep them alive, a place where monitors are so common they seem like robots controlling life. Bob is going there to die. I turn my attention to his son, and beckon Ron to follow me outside Bob's room. He stands in front of me, face-to-face.

"Ron, your Dad has a significant bleed in his brain. The blood you've noticed in different places on his body, and the bleeding in his retina, are all part of the same process." I slow the pace of my words. "Basically, his whole body is hemorrhaging. He is being transferred to ICU, but Ron, this is it. Your Dad isn't going to make it." Bob's son is a big man, strong like his father, and like his father his tears are small drops of pain.

* * *

We sit outside ICU while the staff disappears through the doors with Bob lying in the hospital bed, bags hanging from silver poles, seemingly unaware of any activity around him. His heart beats, but his senses show nothing, no movement in a limb, no twitch in an eye, no smile, no grimace. Nothing.

Our family doctor's cell number is my first call.

"Dr. Bae, it's me, Jeanette."

"How is he doing?"

"He's hemorrhaging. In his brain." We speak in staccato sentences.

"I'm at the office. I'll be right over." The call is complete.

A doctor emerges from the huge ICU doors, crisp in his greens, pensive in his expression. He is average in height, yet dwarfed by Ron's large chest and muscles that look as if they could pump a Volkswagen. The physician introduces himself with words. Extending a hand in a hospital is uncommon, if not hazardous. No one needs to distribute bacteria, but a lack of handshakes also maintains a distance. Too much kindness might crack armors built for the purpose of staying focused, staying steady.

"Mrs. Reese?" he already knows who I am. I am the only woman sitting, waiting at the door of ICU.

"Yes, I'm Jeanette Reese, Bob Canady's wife. This is his son, Ron."

"Hello, nice to meet both of you." I am ready to skip the niceties. "I'm Doctor Avery. I am very sorry to have to share this with you, but your husband's hemorrhage is quite severe. He cannot recover from this, so it will be a matter of hours."

"That's what I've been told by the physician on his case." I proceed to share Bob's diagnosis, his recent bout with pneumonia, his confusion, his medications as though I was one of Bob's physicians. Speaking "doctor" is the resulting curse of too many medical problems, having worked in medical centers, and having cared for family with complex health issues. My own physicians have become extended family in an oddly medical, but emotionally reassuring way.

"I was just reviewing the CAT scan. Do you want to see it?" He gets I understand medical lingo. What he does not get is I cannot look at my husband's brain full of blood.

I pause. "I'm not sure."

Ron turns and looks at the doctor. "I'd like to see it."

My mind wonders how this CAT scan will be different from the other brain scans I have seen in my life. It takes a moment, but I decide I need tangible proof so my heart can let go. "Ron, if you want to look at it, then I will, too."

Dr. Avery punches the button on the side of the ICU entrance, and both doors swing open. He leads us to the X-ray display, and sits down in a simple, mobile chair at the slender table below the display. Ron and I stand behind him.

Bob's scan is still clipped onto the box full of light, waiting for more eyes to peer into his dying brain. I take a deep breath, but forget to exhale, and I look directly at the scan. There is my husband's skull, the very bone which wraps around his brain, the bone which protects this fragile, intelligent organ. Inside the skull there is only black.

"Mrs. Reese, the bleed inside your husband's head is so profuse, it has pushed part of his brain through the base of his skull."

"Oh, my God." The air in my lungs slips out, my tensed shoulders curl forward, and my eyes focus briefly on the floor. *How did this happen?* I wonder, yet I know. Leukemia. Low platelet count. Blood that can't clot. Yes, I know.

The doctor turns around to look at me. "This must be phenomenally painful for your husband."

Phenomenally painful. It seems these words should never be said. It seems these words should never be heard. But I know, with dread sitting at the door of my heart, these words will find a permanent home in my own brain from this moment until my own breath ceases.

The ICU nurse takes us into Bob's private room, with walls that provide separation from other patients so much so it resembles a private high tech hotel room, complete with a view of Newport Harbor, blue water, sail boats, and people strolling outside.

The nurse asks if I would like her to pull the blinds.

"Can people see in?"

"Not now, but they will be able to when the sun sets."

"Then, no, let's not pull the blinds yet." Bob cannot see the harbor, but the beauty of the water is settling, and adds a sense of holiness to this torture. It occurs to me birth and death are the same spiritual process, one coming into this life, the other leaving it. One filled with joy, the other with sadness. They are both gifts that test us, provoking our hearts to reach into the sky and feel the heavens. Death brings us closer to God.

* * *

For a moment, I slip into another time, some weeks earlier. Bob and I were lying on our bed at home, having a conversation about the existence of an afterlife. For some time, he has believed in reincarnation. If evolution is the law of life, of the universe, he reasoned, why would souls not evolve as well? I came into this life with a sense of an ongoing spiritual process. Bob came to his own beliefs through reading about unusual case histories which seemed to offer no other explanation.

That night, as he talked about what was beyond death's door, I suddenly interrupted him.

"Bob, will you wait for me?" He turned his head and looked at me, puzzled at first, eyebrows furrowed downward. "Will you wait for me after you die so we can have another life together?"

His skin took on a subtle glow as he smiled. "I promise."

* * *

The nurse's voice shakes me out of my memory, back into the harshness of today. She looks at Bob. "He's not comfortable. I am going to get some morphine for your husband's IV."

I shake my head slowly. "No, you are not going to give him morphine." The nurse turns toward me, startled by my response. "You are going to give him dilaudid."

"Why do you say that?"

"Because his pain receptors respond better to dilaudid. I don't know why. They just do."

"Then dilaudid it is. It's a stronger drug. We'll keep giving it to him until he is visibly comfortable. I'll be back shortly." There is fluidity in our dance. She responds gracefully to my lead, and I am so grateful.

At 6:00 PM, a staff member opens the glass doors that partition our private room from the hallway's traffic pattern of nurses, physicians and orderlies. She wheels in a small stainless steel table, but there is no monitor, no medical instruments, no syringes. The table is covered with a small, white table cloth and trays of sandwiches, chips and cookies, with bottles of water and juice, and a pot of freshly brewed coffee. The staff brings little rays of light into dark days with simple touches. Bob's son and I both smile and thank her.

As she exits, Dr. Bae arrives. "How's he doing?" He has a pensive look on his face, the one he wears when assessing a situation. He walks over to Bob, gently touching his arm much the way he touches Mother when he queries her for medical data. Connection for this man is as natural as an ocean wave. Dr. Bae touches hearts.

I give him the quick medical update and pause. Neither of us state how little time there is left. For the moment, we both sense the truth is best left silent.

The nurse returns with the first dose of dilaudid. The medication helps Bob's body relax, while the monitors hold steady. Dr. Bae and I watch the electronics beep regular rhythms, charts of light dashing across the screens. I realize these machines offer the last way my husband's severely damaged brain can communicate. *Oh, God, his beautiful mind is gone.*

We eat, we talk, we notice the sun has fallen, and people can peer in the window now, so I pull the blinds and block out the beautiful bay lest our private drama becomes public. I can hardly stand the thought of a stranger, friend or even family member, seeing Bob in this state. This morning, he was Bob. He looked like Bob. But once his cranium filled with blood, and forced his brain into hiding, his physical features changed. Cheeks drawn and gaunt, chin dropped and mouth open, his face transformed into a ghost-like figure reminiscent of Munch's painting, The Scream. The nightmares I had as a child came back to my conscious mind when I saw the painting on a museum wall in Norway. Art foreshadows life. So do nightmares.

Dr. Bae returns to his office while Ron stands on Bob's right, me at Bob's left, each holding a muscular hand turned limp. We must let family know his condition is beyond optimism now, so we divide up the calls. Ron calls his brother and sister; I call Bob's sisters. Friends, parents of two beautiful daughters we consider family, unaware of the sudden turn, text they would like to come to the hospital to visit Bob. My return text is short: *Don't come. In ICU. He is dying now.*

Their 10-year-old texts back: *I am so sad that my heart hurts, and I am crying real tears.* Allyson always loved Bob, so I save her sweet words on my phone.

Suddenly, Bob gasps, the screens on his monitors bounce with activity, and his son bursts into tears, shoulders slumping over while his back moves with the rhythm of his sobs. The power of this scene draws my heart in. The monitors quiet as though listening to our unspoken plea. While a sense of normalcy returns, Bob's vitals are weaker.

I take one last picture of father and son, but the image startles me, still unaccustomed to the changes in Bob's face. Yet, it is my futile attempt to prevent time from moving forward. I cannot hold this moment in perpetuity. Pixels are not permanent.

I do not know how to talk to God in the face of my husband's death. For what shall I pray? That he lives, because *I* do not want to say goodbye? The thought leaves me hollow inside as though a spiritual thirst is left unquenched. What does God want of me? Suddenly, I sense it. *This is not about you, Jeanette. It is about Bob. This is his path, his journey. It is time to let him go.* A peace settles into my soul, allowing me greater focus, and bolsters my waning courage. I can let go. I must.

This strength sustains me as Bob's body drives the monitors into a false—yet all too real—frenzy, a second time, then a third. Minutes pass and the graphs on the screens slow, but this time is different. The lines on the graphs go flat, blending together at their respective baselines. My husband grows still. His lungs do not reach for air. He has flatlined, and the monitors sound their respective alarms announcing his death. Now, I can cry, so I do.

The nurse rushes in and glances at the monitors. This must be a common process for her, one she does daily, if not multiple times throughout a day working in ICU. For me, this is a new process, unaccustomed to people I love dying in a hospital. My family members have died at home, in peace. But I am relieved Bob is in the hospital as the pain was beyond reach, beyond what I would want treated at home. His agony would have consumed me.

Ron and I stand by his side, and as the tears falling down our faces begin to slow, I can see Ron is ready to leave. "Once the person is gone, I'm done. I have no need to sit here with Dad. You go ahead, Jeanette. I'll be in the waiting room. Take your time."

The nurse leaves to give me the private moments I need with Bob. It has been days since I have been able to hold my husband, doctors fearful my flu might be different than the virus which caused his pneumonia. The same fears drove my behaviors, and I have kept a certain distance, unless gloved and gowned like a physician prepared for surgery. Now, I climb onto the bed, and wrap my arms around the man I so love, finally able to lend comfort, but the comfort is only mine. I whisper to him, and stroke his quiet, masculine arm.

An ICU physician walks in the room, apologizing for the interference, explaining he must declare a time of death. "I understand," I tell him, and I sit up, but I do not get off the bed. He works around me, confirms the nurse's assessment, and calls the time of death at 11:36 PM, then quietly leaves the room.

Now, in the privacy of this room by the bay, I talk to Bob about our life together, and try to make up for the lack of touch, the lack of privacy during the last week of his life. I thank him for all he has done for my mother, for all the love we shared. I tell him he is, and always will be, the soul that merged with my soul in this life. I thank him for this gift. Now, I must leave. As I gather my purse and coat, I turn to look back at him one last time.

"Bob, I love you. I'll see you in the next life."

Messages
May 2011

I can barely stand the thought of telling my mother her son-in-law passed away. I visited her the day he died, but my heart would not allow my mouth to utter such words. I know I must find a way to tell my mother about Bob. Even with a diminished memory she always knew Bob. He was the one who got up early every morning, made her coffee, then sat and ate with her for the fourteen years she lived with us. He was the one who took care of her car. He was the one she deemed always right regardless of the topic of conversation between Bob and me. Mom knew she did not have to agree with her daughter. My love was undying. But she was not about to risk Bob's affection.

Mom had consented to moving into a facility when Bob started his cancer treatment. After four months, she begged me to take her out. She wanted to be back home, with us, in a place where she felt whole. Still facing neck surgery, I was not strong enough to care for Bob and manage mother's care as well. Yet now, I have to be strong enough to tell my sweet mother her wonderful son-in-law died yesterday.

I open the door of the facility, sign in, and start toward the lunchroom. The hallways always smell fresh; the carpet always appear clean. The lunchroom is large enough to hold almost fifty people, and seven or eight caregivers energize the room as they pass out plates of food while speaking cheerfully to the residents. I visit four or five times a week, almost always at lunch. Mother can no longer feed herself, which allows me the opportunity to feed her the way she fed me so many years before, bonding yet again—this time our roles reversed.

She sits at her assigned table quietly with five or six other residents, most of whom are unable to speak, or perhaps unwilling. Their eyes are cast downward, their moods even lower. I wonder how deeply boredom permeates their cells. It is that way for Mother. She, unlike most of the others, has Parkinson's with dementia. She understands a considerable amount, but her brain cannot direct her speech to something flowing, to something intelligible, so her words are like a salad being tossed in a large bowl. At times, Mother would shake her head in disbelief with the concoctions that came out of her mouth. She had not completed a sentence in weeks.

Her soft-boned back is bent over like a tree which had been blown by strong winds since a seedling. Her eyes, too, cast more downward than forward. She cannot see me well in her position, so I plant a kiss on her cheek and ask, "How are you doing, Mom?" She assures me in her simple words she is fine. She never complains. She never wants me to worry. I never stop.

There is a stool next to her wheelchair large enough to sit on, small enough to nestle in close to her side. The stool allows me to sit slightly behind her, enabling me to more easily navigate food from her plate to her mouth. I look up as one of the caregivers, plumpish in stature with a gentle smile, and hair richer than brown, waves to me. She asks, "Hi, Jeanette. How is your husband?" Even the caregivers at the facility have a great affection for Bob. I get up and carefully stand behind my mother.

"I'm fine. How are you?" Shaking my head while pointing to Mother, I put my finger up to my mouth to quiet the caregiver, silently mouthing, "He didn't make it." She understands. Mother does not know yet. I have to prepare to tell Mother, and a lunchroom filled with fifty some residents is not a kind place to share shattering news.

Besides, Bob had vanished from this plane of my world less than twelve hours before, yet I can still feel his presence as though he stands behind me gently exhaling on my neck to comfort me. I cannot even utter the words "Bob" and "died" in the same sentence for fear of my throat closing only to choke off my air. It is imperative to maintain my composure when I tell Mother. She will need my support. But I have to control my thoughts to control my composure, which is a hellishly hard task from moment to moment.

The caregiver walks across the room, around the table, silently stands behind Mother, and extends her arms toward me. Without words, I stand there while her arms wrap around my slender frame. I sit back down on the stool, drape my arm around Mom's shoulder, and begin to say something, anything, to refocus my thoughts on my mother—still on hospice herself—and off my husband. Moving the bench closer to the table to see her face, I gently kiss her forehead. My mind, so blurred by the fog of grief, wonders, *how will I tell her Bob is gone?* My thought is interrupted. Mother has something to say.

She looks down into her lap, so very quietly. "I already knew that, Jeanette."

"Mom, what did you say?"

"I already knew it."

No more words pass through her lips. Squirming in my seat, I fumble in my attempt to avoid her message, as bold and brave as it was. I lack the courage my tiny, bent-over, rarely verbal Mother has. It took me one more day to tell her that her darling son-in-law had passed, something she already knew.

How could she have known?

Then I remember what happened when Ed, one of Bob's dearest friends, died with an unfinished task.

It was three years ago when Bob received a voice mail from Ed, a kindly, elegant gentleman, who quietly summoned the courage required to face end-stage cancer. Ed knew his time was near. He called to tell Bob goodbye. Bob, traveling up the coast to a board meeting, had no cell coverage for an hour or two and missed the call. By the time he was able to check messages and return the call, Ed had slipped into a coma. Bob, tears in his eyes, went to bed for a fitful sleep.

During the night, as he described it, a luminous light some eighteen inches from his face awakened him shining intensely in his eyes. Bob stared into the light hovering above him for thirty or forty seconds, and watched as it slowly withdrew, suddenly evaporating into the night. Bob told me he shook his head questioning his own senses, then looked at the clock. It was 1:30 AM. A feeling of peace spread through his body taking him into a deep slumber.

The next morning, he got the call. Ed had passed. During the night. At 1:30 AM.

So how did my mother know Bob had died?

I can't answer that question. I simply do not know. But it does make me wonder if love can cross the boundaries of life. And if Bob's love crosses the thin line between life and death, perhaps it is unencumbered by a human artifact called time.

Missing Data
May 2011

"Should something happen to me, everything you need is right in this notebook. My financial information, my military information—everything." Bob held the white, three-ring binder in his hand and walked me through the summary page.

It has been ten days since he died, yet I remembered the conversation so clearly, as though his words still floated in the air. I miss his voice, his laughter, even his thoughtful silence so full of meaning.

But I have a task at hand. I must integrate all our accounts now, and none of his financial data is in the notebook. It is not what I anticipated, certainly not what he told me. It seems I have met an unexpected reality.

Keli arrives to help me organize the files and papers and piles of documents. She picks up Bob's notebook and turns each page examining the words and numbers carefully. I trust her with my financial data. Why would I not? I trusted her to care for my husband while I cared for my mother, reversing roles as needed. Numbers are far less important than hearts.

"Keli, I know he prepared all this information for me. I'm sure that's what he meant when he said everything was in this book."

"I don't see it anywhere, Jeanette." She looks up and I see her brow rise, then deepen into a frown as she cocks her head. "It doesn't make sense. Where is the financial information?" She picks up another binder and begins to flip through its pages. There are files littered throughout the office, most sitting on a table in the center of the room. Keli slowly lowers herself into Bob's desk chair. "I wonder what happened."

"It's got to be here somewhere. He certainly gave me that impression, but I can't even find a file on his computer." I managed our mutual and my business account. He managed his business account, and a mutual savings account. "I know one account is at the local bank, Keli, but I am not sure if he has more than two. He changed banks a couple of times. And there should be some old life insurance policies. I haven't a clue where they are or if they are active."

There has to be an explanation, one of logic, one of sense. But the gracious widow I hope to be slips into a being for whom I have little affection as I realize my husband had not completed the process to remove his ex-wife of many years earlier from the life insurance policy. After tracking his steps, I understood how the error was made. A change in beneficiary required one last form beyond all the changes he had made. Just one. Even though his ex-wife relinquished ownership of all the life insurance policies—clearly documented in his ancient divorce decree—a name on a beneficiary list trumps all other legal documents. She got the check. It was not a large amount, but I still suspect my husband kicked the inside of his casket.

"How the hell did he forget the financial data? Bob ran businesses, multi-million dollar budgets! He had two masters degrees and a doctorate. I truly don't understand how he let this happen."

My hands clench and my long nails etch marks in my palms. I am angry I must focus on financial problems which should have been addressed prior to his passing. I am also selfish. I want to spend this time grieving the man I love. I do not want to spend this time deciphering financial issues. I have no affection for such issues. None.

Keli watches me, her body leaning against the back of Bob's chair. It seems oversized holding her slender body. "Keli, it just doesn't seem like Bob."

"You're right. It doesn't seem typical of Bob. When did you review the notebook the first time?"

"A year or so ago. I was so sure I saw his bank account and insurance information listed on the first page in the binder."

"No, I mean after Bob died. How much time elapsed before you opened this?" She pointed her finger at the binder.

"Oh. Well, I took it out of the bookcase and set it on this table, but I didn't want to take the time to read it when I had guests. I opened it after everyone had headed back home."

Keli looked up from the book. "So that would be about seven or eight days after Bob passed?"

"Right. Maybe Bob took it out for some reason. Just makes no sense."

The next day's search is much the same. We search file cabinets, folders, his office drawer. We find statements from closed accounts, statements from accounts that may be closed, but require calls to banks—banks that do not want to speak to someone not listed on the account. We find old insurance documents, but this too requires calls. These companies take my call simply because I have an account number. Any less credibility and each call would have been cut off.

"Come on, Keli, let's get in the car and go see Mom. I have to get out of here."

"Would you mind if I dropped you to see your mother and I borrowed your car? I have a couple of things to get done, and I can get you some gas while I'm doing my errands."

My mother waits for me. Each day I arrive, her silence echoes her patience. It has been ten months since I moved Mother from our home to the facility as Bob entered treatment. The building is locked so residents are locked inside, each door leading to nowhere, and each time I visit I want to steal her, and bring her back home. This facility was the best I could find. It is clean. People are kind. I even know the CEO. I still hate it. It somehow adds to my mounting frustration of missing financial data.

The dining room is greenish, carpeted, and cluttered with round tables which accommodate four people. I feed Mother by gently spooning bites of food into her mouth when she finds using a fork on her own too difficult.

Another patient walks by our table. It is not her real name, but she is called "Bill." I stand up to greet her, slip beside her, and place my hand upon her shoulder.

"You look so nice today, Bill." She continues to look straight ahead, her eyes narrowing to a glare, lines on her forehead deepening, then she opens her mouth to respond.

"I AM nice." She pushes my hand from her shoulder with a fast snap of her wrist.

"Well, yes, you are nice. And you are wearing a lovely color today." I know not to touch her again.

Her eyes are still focused forward. Her head lowers on her neck, and she declares, "I'm just going to have to slap the shit out of you!"

Bill is strong—and apparently tough. I am a slender, if not delicate, woman. But she must be close to 85. I doubt she could catch me. So, I bite my tongue to manage my laughter.

"You know what else I like about you, Bill?"

"No! What?" Her sentences are clipped, and end with a point like a pair of scissors.

"You have a great sense of humor."

Her shoulders drop, her steps lighten, but she still does not look at me.

"Oh, okay!" Her voice bounces, and it is over faster than it began. She walks away as though a spring has been planted in each of her heels.

A long lost smile finds my lips. I forget my frustration with bank accounts. I forget my anger with Bob. Momentarily, laughter restores the balance missing in my life since his death. I miss him each minute I am not angry as though life is a seesaw, yet the anger hurts less than the emptiness of our bed.

Keli walks in the door, her steps quick, her smile stuck midway up her cheeks. Her determination seems to vacillate, but it is clear it is time to return home. I turn and lean toward Mother as we share a kiss. She is always a reason to smile.

I look at the pavement as we approach my car. Keli listens as I tell her about Bill and her desire to slap the shit out of me. I laugh, but Keli is restrained and walks with a tenseness in her step. I look up. My pace stops when I see the rear end of my Lexus.

"My God, Keli, someone hit my car!"

She shuddered, then stalled. "I know. I'm so sorry. Someone rear-ended me at a stoplight."

"Oh."

"I really am so sorry, Jeanette." Keli continued to talk without stopping to take a breath. "I know what a frustrating day today has been. The guy just hit me. I have his name, and his phone number, and his insurance information, and I can give you mine, and I will pay for it, and..."

"Keli, are you okay? You're not hurt?"

"No, I'm fine. It's just you have had so much on your plate lately, I didn't want to add to it."

"Well, maybe I just need to sic Bill on the guy who hit my car. She'd know what to do." Keli drew in a deep breath and began to laugh. I inspect the bruised bumper, dents creasing the silver paint, then I start to giggle while both our bodies lean against the strength of the car. I realize there are times when laughter is the only line of defense.

* * *

Back at home, Keli sits at Bob's desk while I sit at mine as we continue our search for financial information. Anger sets in again as I pour through file after file of bank statements, investment statements, and the binder Bob had prepared. I hate being angry with the man I love, even post-mortem, but I am. So very angry. As the steam rises off my shoulders, I ponder Bill's line and look up at the ceiling.

"Bob, I'm just going to have to slap the shit out of you!" I raise my small fists to the heavens, imagining they look menacing. They do not. Bob always laughed when I playfully raised my fists in defiance. He would pull back as though terrified, then burst into laughter. A small woman has to work hard to appear menacing—something I never mastered.

After days of searching, I locate an unmarked thumb drive with a file that has all Bob's financial information. The original document is gone, the original file from his computer is gone, valuable time is lost, but the critical data is here on this simple, unmarked thumb drive. I sigh in relief. Keli begins to laugh, and a bit of balance returns to the office that is, by now, stacked with boxes full of files.

Voices
June 2011

My Sweetest One,
As you may guess, I write to you late at
night and retire with the pleasant
memories of you. God, I would love to see
your smile...even teasing me about
being a Republican.

Robert Canady, May 13, 1995

Voices. I hear voices. It is 3:00 in the morning, and I hear voices downstairs in the room directly below our bedroom. My spine stiffens as I sit straight up in bed. The down comforter, encased in a multi-toned blue cover, slides off my chest. I sleep alone in our queen bed since Bob died six weeks ago. Even if I try to reach over and touch his shoulder to wake him—a simple reflex—his presence in our bed is over forever, like all the words in Webster's that define permanent.

I can't hear what the voices are saying, but they are below me, directly below me and they are loud, almost as if fighting.

My mind retraces the steps I repeat each night before getting in bed. Earlier that evening, I latched the windows tightly as if to warn intruders this home does not welcome them. I checked the house doors, all securely locked, most double locked with deadbolts. The door from the side yard into the garage was bolted tight enough to be glued shut. That sense of glue holds me together each night, allowing sleep to permeate my body. The alarm did its customary beep when I set it. *So who is talking downstairs?*

There are walls and locks and alarms all around me creating my own safe barricade. The doors must tire of me locking and unlocking them, but one gets used to having a stronger, larger person in the home after so many years of marriage.

The walls must tire of me more, posing and reposing my unanswered questions. *How did this happen? Why did he die?* But I know the science, the medical truth. Dying from leukemia reduced his life to an eight-letter word with such power it can tip life upside down. Not just his life, but mine as well.

What are they saying downstairs? These voices are loud, talking at each other, as though squabbling, jabbing, testing one another. I shake my head slightly, tilting it to listen carefully and somehow the fogginess of sleep is tossed aside. How many burglars would come into a house and initiate what sounds like a family feud afire? *Oh my god, it's the TV!* Suddenly, I feel safe. I know I am safe. No intruder would come into a locked house at 3:00 in the morning to turn on a damn TV.

I get out of bed, walk across the cream carpeting, grasp the bedroom door handle, and listen for the pop as it unlocks. The t-shirt covering my body is tacky and thread-worn, and before I begin my walk downstairs wondering if I should cover myself with my white robe. *What for? It's just the TV!*

I'm not a big fan of the HD widescreen my husband purchased. Not that I have issues with televisions, but TV and computer screens are like magnets with seductive spin, engaging email, and questionably fabulous Facebook pages. My husband loved them. To me they stole time from us, the two of us together, when there was so little time left. The worst time thief was Fox News. I began to dislike squabbling O'Reilly. When Bob passed, I deleted the scheduled tapings of all the Fox shows. I no longer turned on the set to find myself face-to-face with angry Glenn Beck. I no longer had to hear Fox at a volume that worked for my husband's fading hearing, but pounded on my own eardrums. Perhaps the only positive about my husband's passing is I gained control of the remote.

My insides still ache wondering if some part of him lingers on within the walls of our home. I hope for a sign, some simple little sign, he will stay by me to help me get through this pain. It is the way of grief. It was the same when my first husband died. Grief charts its own course, and those of us remaining on this plane of existence are left behind to follow grief's path. I prefer driving.

I begin to walk downstairs, steadying myself, holding the wood railings lining the staircase, slowly placing my white-socked toes on each step at a pace reminiscent of a stroll through a park. Pausing at the landing, I become fully aware I had turned off the television before coming to bed leaving the screen as black as black paint, the blue light on the Direct TV box dark. *Who turned on the television?*

I listen again. There is something familiar in the way these voices speak to each other. *Oh, my God. I think the television is on Fox News!* My legs hesitate no more, and I walk into the family room. Yes, it's Fox News. I smile, perhaps for the first time ever while watching Fox. The remote sits on the table next to Bob's easy chair, his pillow still plumped up and in place. I haven't disturbed his space, hoping some part of him will stay close so the ache in my heart is more bearable. I pick up the remote, watch Fox for ten seconds, and look back at his chair. Fox News, middle of the night, loud enough to wake the neighbors? I smile.

Okay, Bob, you made your point.

Coming Home
November 2011

Mother has been in this dementia facility for fourteen months now, and each visit with her becomes more difficult. When I look at her, I see a full heart, one that radiates love. I see a woman who still understands and responds to the pain of others, a woman who still wants to interact, despite her speech difficulties. When the staff looks at her, they see a woman who cannot eat on her own nor communicate well, so they leave her with patients who can do little more than simply stare into space, unable to interact, unaware of their surroundings. It is how we differ, the staff and I. I see capabilities. They see disabilities. It is hard to watch.

They mean well, but they do not understand her complex medical case, and they miss important details. I remember the team member who came to our home as part of the intake interview. I set our caregiver charts on the table in front of her, and explained why it was so important to record how much liquid Mother took in as well as her level of output. She had been close to death twice due to bladder and kidney issues. I stressed tracking her food intake was critical as well. Sometimes, her colon would shut down with life threatening blockages. The doctors had managed to save her each time, and each time warned me we might lose her. Our in-home caregivers completed the charts daily, knowing I would review the records regularly. It was the only way, I explained, to catch these problems before it was too late.

Her long term physicians trusted my understanding of medicine, most notably when it came to Mother's case. When a new neurosurgeon decided she needed brain surgery to reduce fluid on her brain in hopes of reducing her

133

dementia, I questioned him. "So you are willing to put her under general anesthesia, which increases the rate of dementia, to draw fluid off her brain to decrease her dementia?"

He stalled, sputtered, then declared, "Well, if she were my mother, I'd do it."

I told him I would think about his recommendation, and as Mother and I rose to leave I noticed her bladder had let loose on his couch. I graciously apologized, but secretly wanted to pat her on the back and say, "Way to go, Mom!" We never returned.

My mother's neurologist sided with me when I recalled the story to him, stating, "That guy is knife happy, Jeanette." The same thought had occurred to me.

My knowledge of her condition allowed me to fine-tune the training of our live-in caregivers, so when the facility intake worker assured me their team would follow my lead, I was able to breathe easier letting Mother go.

But they did not follow my lead. All the directions I posted for them on the wall by her bed were removed within three days. I was informed, with a smile, they knew how to do their job.

They did, as simple caregiving goes, but they did not understand the medical complexities of Mother's case. She ended up in the hospital with a grand mal seizure from severe dehydration. The fluids I asked them to track were the fluids they chose not to chart. A week later, she had another seizure so severe it took the medical team at the hospital 45 minutes to control.

Part of the issue was the internal communication in the facility. The caregivers could not even read their own charts about Mother, and the head nurse readily admitted the confusion to me. I discovered she never even reported the seizures to the administrator. I was stunned. She was fired. I knew the other facilities in town. I had interviewed them. Mother was in the best one in town, but she was beyond their level of care, and they did not understand that simple fact.

When Mother moved into the facility, she had a roommate, a woman who was nice to me, but who was stuck in a rewinding of life. The roommate had Alzheimer's which slowly reverses the many psychological stages of human development until one stalls in a perpetual state of baby-hood, lying listlessly on a bed essentially unable to respond. One day as I walked Mother around the facility, the roommate and her girlfriend walked by us, one pointing at Mom bent over her walker, whispering to the other in less than a quiet voice, "We don't want to be around her."

Emotions whirl at such a comment. I felt sad for these two women travelling back in time through the ugly teen years, yet like a lioness with a cub, I wanted to scratch someone with a claw. I put my hand on Mother's back, and held my head high with pride. I do not know if Mother's heart was seared the way mine was, but her gentle dignity would have hidden it from view.

During the time when Bob was very ill, Mother developed a friendship with a gentleman named Ben. He was kind, and looked at my mother with soft, blue eyes. They sat together every day at mealtime. One day as I entered the facility, a lovely older woman approached me. "Are you Elma's daughter?"

"Why yes, I am."

Her voice was gentle. "My name is Eve." A slender woman, Eve stood there initially hesitant, then the words spilled from her lips. "My husband is in love with your mother."

"Oh. Your husband must be Ben."

She nodded.

"Ben is so kind to my mother." I watched for any changes in her expression which might be a clue. "Are you okay with this, Eve?"

She faced me. "Oh yes, his mind left me some time ago. I am so pleased he found someone here. He has been so lonely, but I couldn't care for him any longer." Eve looked older and frail. "I'm moving Ben to a facility closer to my home. He'll be leaving as soon as there is an opening."

I could already feel the pain in Mother's heart. It took her weeks to get over Paul when his family suddenly moved him to Northern California to be with his daughter, but her support system was whole and intact. Now she will lose Ben, the only friend in this community where minds slowly lose connection with the world.

After Ben left, Mother grieved. She missed the one kind face that loved to sit with her, and as much as they were able, to notice each other as people. They had smiled more together, held hands, and helped each other feel human again. After Ben left, I wondered if he could find another Elma to lessen his pain.

Fortunately for Mother a lovely woman named Pat befriended her. Pat's short hair was a brilliant red; and she waddled, her weight causing her to sway side-to-side as she ambled down the hall pushing her walker. Her blue eyes sparkled whenever she saw Mother. Mother loved her kindness as Pat would help her eat when the tremors shook Mom's hands. After a while, the caregivers refused to let Mother eat with Pat, who had more control managing her own fork. Helping others was stressful for Pat, they told me. I only saw the love in Pat's eyes for her dear friend, Elma.

I fought for Mother to be able to continue to sit with the more capable residents, ones who could speak, residents who treated Mother with love, but it took too much time for the caregivers to feed my mother when other residents needed their plates delivered to their tables, so they moved her to a dining area with residents who sat silently, heads lowered, drool dripping from their mouths. They explained to me since Mother had no sense of concepts, interaction was not critical, and here, in what *I* considered to be the dining room for the dying, she could be watched more closely.

* * *

Hours later as we traverse the halls, Mother seems down as her steps are slower today, and she rarely glances up at people. She looks at the floor, and in a listless voice tells me, "I just want to die." I share the comment with her caregiver who informs me she has heard such comments, too. This information stops the administrator in her tracks.

"Oh my God, your mother understands concepts."

I know it. Her caregiver knows it, but no one with any authority seems willing to see the totality of the little human being in front of me. I have had enough.

"Mom, I have to have neck surgery in a few days. After that, I can't come to visit for two or three weeks, but when I can, I am taking you back home to live with me."

She looks up at me like a small child who has found her once-lost mother. She knows I will keep my word. Miss Elma smiles at me with a hope in her eyes, a hope I have not seen in months, and she radiates quiet warmth as the small wrinkles around her eyes gently dance on her cheekbones. I cannot wait to have her home again.

* * *

The surgery is a tough one, requiring two extra days in the hospital. The neck brace extends from my breast bone to my chin in the front, and from my shoulder blades to the base of my skull in the back. There will be no turning of my neck for weeks: no ups, no downs, no sideways, just straight ahead. I drive with a special mirror which allows me to see 180 degrees—from side-to-side and everything behind me. An accident could be catastrophic with a neck not fully healed, so I drive as little as possible.

The Monday after Thanksgiving, I stand at the facility front door with Mother's new live-in caregiver, Zena, and Keli who always finds her way back to town if she suspects I need help. Zena is from the Philippines, and her long, straight black hair falls down her back. She appears to be 28 or so, but her DNA does not seem to understand how to age. I am astonished to learn she is 46. She arrived from Arizona yesterday, and helped me transform the dining room into a hospital room with a hospital bed, a twin bed for her, and Mother's two pink dressers. We hung bath curtains between the dining room and the living room so people outside will not be able to peer into the private dining-room-turned-bedroom.

We arrive to find the facility has Mother's belongings packed. Elizabeth, Mom's caregiver, tears up, so I promise to invite her to lunch so she can see Mother again. She needs to know, to be very sure, Mother has quality care at home. She, too, has assumed the role of daughter. Most of the staff has warmed to Mother, as few hearts can turn away from the warmth of such a sun. We tour the corridors, stopping to say goodbye at the nurse's station, wishing caregivers well, and catching residents roaming the facility. Now Mother's belongings are loaded in the car, and we help her climb into the front seat. I cannot wait to get on the freeway.

Her vertebrae have slowly collapsed over time, so she is so short her once 5'2" frame now only reaches 4'7".

Miss Elma may have the spine of an old woman, but her eyes are the eyes of a child trying to peer over the dashboard to see everything she can as we whiz down the freeway. Her dark pupils are as big as the moon, and she stretches her spine as tall as she can, mouth agape as though everything she sees is new when nothing is really new at all. She is so cute Zena and Keli laugh.

I smile. I reach over and pat her lovely little hand. "Mom, we're taking you home. You're coming home to stay. For good."

Nothing can make this a better day.

Best Friends
March 2012

My Bob would have been 82 years-young today. It is a day on the calendar I wanted to skip, but time has its own rules, and it moves forward each day pulling me right along—most of the time willingly, sometimes not.

I wonder if anyone else remembered today is Bob's birthday, so I venture to his computer and open his Facebook page, a page I should have taken down by now, but I hold onto pieces of life treating each like a photograph so people and memories won't fade away. This is just one more. Today, I find multiple postings wishing Bob, wherever he is, a nice birthday.

Many refer to him as a best friend. No one, save me, ever knew Bob admitted to having just two best friends, but his kindness touched everyone around him. It was not that he did not love many people, because he did. But to Bob a best friend was a different category, one of growing up together or running a business together, relationships which were tested but where loyalty triumphed. Some days, when the grief seeps into my core and controls my thoughts, I cannot help but wonder how I fit in his life. The crushing pain hits fast, eyes tear rapidly, then suddenly dry up like a well in a desert. The crying always stops sooner or later.

The day is bright and the air crisp as I walk outside to pick up the mail. I pull the five-by-seven envelope from my small, but clumsy mailbox sitting precariously atop a white post in front of our house. I know I should get this stabilized one day, but like the cluttered garage, the broken backyard swing, and the notes of condolences, projects sit as though in a deep, sound sleep. If I write a thank you note, I will surely wake the dead.

The writing on the envelope is unfamiliar, but the return address is not. The envelope is from Georgia. It is from one of my husband's cousins, a unique, kind man to whom Bob was very special. It is the size of a card. *Oh, he is acknowledging me on Bob's birthday! How nice of him.*

I slide my finger along the back of the envelope to pull the flap loose. I remove the contents. This is not a commercial card for me. The entire front cover is a photo of Bob's face with his name, date of birth, and date of death at the very bottom. It is a picture. No, this is not a picture. It is an invitation, an invitation to a family reunion. Bob has followers—if not disciples.

* * *

Seeing the invitation triggers memories from one of the events I held in honor of him a month after he died, his Celebration of Life. It was a public honoring of Bob and his contributions, and held at a friend's home on a hill overlooking the tops of trees and the city below. Those attending were not his "folks," family and friends from Georgia, but professional friends for whom he had a genuine fondness. Once the scheduled speakers finished, one after the other stood up, unsolicited, and spoke about Bob. I felt so honored so many friends cared so much. His public persona was so strong.

* * *

I look down at the invitation in my hand, and unwelcome feelings slip up my chest and into the back of my throat. I flip the picture over so I do not have to look at it. My action stuns me as I experience an odd emotion I have felt so rarely, I must stop and consider it to give it a name. *Ah, yes, jealousy.* I cannot seem to balance this unattractive emotion with the flashes of anger that he's gone. *How dare he die.*

I know anger is so often part of healing. It hides my grief, but also my hurt. And I do feel hurt. I learned to store old hurts as a child, so I turn this less-than-effective skill on my departed husband. Old anger bubbles up to my consciousness. I can still see him leaning against the bathroom sink, irritated by some comment I made, which by now has vanished from my mind. He needed to bare his soul, and in doing so he was prone to dump a truck load of "stuff." I question he meant to hurt me, but my doubts still haunt me like a ghost of fears past. I am unsure how he would describe my efforts to deal with difficult emotions, although he might have described me as having an occasional problem with cleats on the end of my tongue. Some friends would be surprised we had testy conversations. My fear is singular: is it possible to speak honestly about a man with a godlike reputation? What disciples do not realize is "gods" are human. Bob loved deeply, his compassion was unending, and he could be as grumpy and testy as any other person.

If he were here now, I would ask, "Did you love me? If you did, why did you make me feel less important?" I suspect he would have wondered how I *could* feel less important. *Why did I not ask some of these questions before?* Oh yes, it made more steam lift off his ears.

The hurt I feel now clouds my ability to own my emotional "stuff." What was *he* feeling? He did give me a clue one day, one I ignored, even discounted; yet one I had no right to disregard.

"Jeanette," I knew he was about to say something important when he used my name. "Nothing I do is ever good enough for you." He had that look he used when he wanted to appear tough, even a little mean.

"How can you say that, Honey? I think you're great." Compliments are poor diversions from the truth. Even as I spoke I could feel the lie deep within me, so deep I could not hear it whispering to me. He was great, yet I did criticize the little things, the things that do not matter in life. *But they do matter.* Each criticism chipped at the love for me behind his blue eyes. I could not feel the hurt in his heart. I could not see the hurt in his eyes. Perhaps I just could not see.

Looking back, I wonder, did we let the day-to-day stresses of life come between us? Is grief distorting my memory?

Did he think I didn't love him?

I need a break from this thinking, this wondering, this regurgitating, so I sit down in front of the television. The program airing is about a wife who has lost her husband, a popular man, one who had counseled many people, many of them her own friends. When the wife speaks at the funeral there are enough tears to turn a creek into a river. She cries. Her friends cry. I roll my eyes. *This is so melodramatic!*

During the commercial, I glance at the picture of Bob on the bookshelf next to the television. I suddenly realize it is the same picture as the one sitting on my bathroom counter, the same one sitting on my desk, and the same one sitting on the piano in the living room. The only room that doesn't have that picture is the kitchen. *My, God, I've built a shrine to Bob.* I begin to cry. I cry more than the drama queen on *Desperate Housewives*. Oh, God.

I pick up my phone and look at the photo of Bob laying on the couch, pillow plumped behind his head, and his body wrapped tightly in his USC snuggly smiling like a little kid who had found a piece of candy. I have turned my husband into a wallpaper display on my cell phone. But the picture is getting little white spots around his eyes, which makes me wonder if the pixels are dying and the picture will fade away. I turn the phone off and on again, even drop it on the floor to shock the pixels back into life, demanding each pixel return and fully restore Bob's face. *You can't fade away. You haven't even been dead a year.*

I hate living with this angst. The ups, the downs. I love Bob, but I am angry. I adore his disciples, but I am envious. What am I missing? What have I yet to learn?

I look up to the ceiling. *Bob, help me understand!*

A memory begins to emerge, one from eighteen years ago, a time when I knew little of Bob Canady. My husband, Jack, was dying. As I tried to build my consulting business—helping organizations chart their future—Bob offered his time as a "shadow consultant," a behind-the-scenes coach to guide me through the challenges of my client's organization. It helped to have two sets of eyes, and a bit of calmness returned to my life in the midst of losing my husband. Bob refused to let me pay him. He just wanted to help.

Each week I looked forward to his call. Bob's first question was always about my husband. The second question was always about me.

If he heard a waiver or slight shiver in my words, I would hear his soft voice at the end of the line encouraging me to make a list of what I needed to do, reassuring me he would call back later to help me prioritize. I was unnerved my armor cracked, and pieces seemed to crumble to the floor at times. It was as though Bob could reach through the phone lines, scoop me up, along with my broken armor and all its pieces, and set me back in my chair.

Here was this man, this man I barely knew, offering kindnesses a best friend would offer. His kindness embarrassed me, knowing my pain leaked through my public persona. His kindness cradled me when there was no net to catch me. His kindness charmed me when my heart was dying with the loss of my first husband.

And after Jack's passing, Bob's kindness led me down a path of falling in love with my best best friend. I, too, became his disciple.

Happy Birthday, my Love, wherever you are.

The Decision to Donate
June 2012

Now, she is losing ground day by day. Mother has been on hospice longer than the time it took from Bob's diagnosis to the time of his death. Each infection weakens her immune system as does her age. The ground does not stay firm beneath one's feet as we grow older.

Worse yet, Mother's brain is losing control over the most fundamental of bodily functions in a haphazard, startling way. It can no longer control her blood pressure which spikes, then drops. Her pulse and respiration rates fluctuate as well. When I touch her hand to comfort her, it is hot as though it has been baking in an oven. The rest of her body is cool. These changes are courtesy of Parkinson's Disease (PD).

PD takes control of Mother's body so slowly the hospice nurse describes the decline as glacial. It is a hard way to end life.

Miss Elma was smarter than smart, embracing one book after the other. She loved discussing current events, religion and social issues. A few years ago, our minds lived in these worlds and we chatted endlessly. I loved her brain. That is why I decided to donate it for medical research.

Some were curious why I would make such a decision, but I know three other people with PD. One only needs to know one afflicted person to want to stop this disease.

One was a television actor. After noticing his professional photos, I asked if he was THE actor from a popular 70's show. His smile grew wide. Afterwards, he spoke to me regularly until he could no longer speak. Then he simply nodded his head. Before long, he just touched my foot with his walker as he shuffled by. Gene found ways to acknowledge me, ever grateful I had acknowledged him.

The other two people I know with PD are resilient women I am honored to call friends. I see how they fight with such dignity. They, too, are smart people, women with heart. One sits in a wheel chair, and in a Parkinson's whisper she expresses more concern for my mother than for herself. She still delivers one-liners which send me rolling off a chair.

The other friend with PD still coaches tennis, refusing to relinquish the normalcy of life. She totters a bit as she walks, and too often her steps are accompanied by pain, but that does not stop her. She still travels the world, a photographer that captures the essence of humanity in each face with the simple click of her camera. She holds onto life, tasting its gifts each day. Beautiful brains fight valiantly.

As I watch these four people who have touched my life, I ask myself how can I help? I read more about medical research and Parkinson's. I learn that to understand this devastating disease, science must look at brains laced with the changes of PD—a compelling reason to donate Mother's beautiful brain to science.

Even though Mother was declared incompetent, and she left me in charge of her healthcare, I do not own Miss Elma. She has three more children. To me, the gifting of a brain goes beyond legal boundaries and passes into causeways of compassion and family dynamics.

I call each sibling, share my observations about the devastation of this disease, and explain the one way science could help other PD patients is to examine the brains of those who have passed, those who lost the fight with Parkinson's. I truly believe Miss Elma would be so proud of this decision. My siblings agree.

Yet, it takes me days to face the internet and initiate this process. I know Mother planned on cremation, as did my father, and even though I know her body will be reduced to ashes when she dies, I wonder what is causing my reticence to pursue the donation more quickly. The truth lies in being able to let go.

But it is not easy to do. I have cared for this woman for fourteen years. I have watched her choke and sputter from swallowing difficulties, and wrestle with tremors which cause her limbs to tremble like a tree shaken at its roots. I have listened as she lost her ability to speak, to say, "I love you."

I am close to letting go, but my ingrained habit of fighting for her life dies hard. I want to tell her everything will be all right, but I do not have the guts to lie. I suspect her courage is bigger than mine.

In my search, I find the Michael J. Fox Foundation for Parkinson's Research. The staff sends me links to organizations in need of brain donations for medical research. After some review, I select a well respected university, pick up the phone, and press each number with an internal hesitance.

The man on the other end of the line is Dr. Rasheed. He is so pleased to get the call, it occurs to me not enough family members and patients realize the importance of post-mortem brain research in search of a Parkinson's cure or even better treatments.

I suspect most people hesitate for the same reason I have. It requires an internal investigation into one's emotions. For me, it also requires a realization that in some deeply resonant way, we are all related, all part of the family of man. That is why we donate hearts, and livers, and kidneys, and yes, brains. It requires more than courage. It requires compassion.

It takes two days of stops and starts to complete the donation paperwork the research team requires. They request Mother's medical history, any MRI's and CT scans available. But I plan to send more, hoping someday, as new evidence emerges, researchers would be able to look back in her file, and tease out an old bit of information that might be key in a new theory.

My strength comes from staying steady on a clinical path, sounding like a hybrid medical student and daughter. Concerned the crematorium could not accommodate the procedure, I naïvely ask questions until this remarkable researcher answers with such clinical detail he moves me to tears. I interrupt him to explain the "daughter" side of me cannot handle this type of information.

I prepare a notebook, complete with dividers creating separate sections for history, medications, etc., and carefully place it in a box. I address it with great care, fighting some irrational fear it might be delivered to the wrong address, or worse, get lost in the mail.

I say little at the post office, setting the package on the counter and debating whether to send it book rate or first class, until I find my center and once again realize the importance of this act, this decision, this trip to the post office. I request first class delivery.

Once I walk out the glass doors, and get in my car, my emotions hit. Tears fall, then a peaceful satisfaction emerges. I call one of my best friends, the husband of my dear friend with Parkinson's. I have to tell him the story, the story of a special donation from an incredibly special mother. My voice tightens in the telling.

He agrees with my siblings. "This is exactly what Elma would want," he tells me.

"I know." And if Parkinson's had not stolen the smile off her face, or robbed her of her beautiful voice, she would tell us herself.

The Turning
December 2012

"Oh, God, I can feel it happening."

My mother is lying in the makeshift hospital room, once my dining room, and I can sense she is going to die soon. It's not as if I don't have objective evidence. The hospice team that normally comes three or four times a week has switched to round-the-clock care today. It penetrates my core, as though a sense of knowingness, a deep sense of intuition, has claimed my body. It owns me now.

* * *

Eighteen months ago I sat with my husband in ICU, watching him die as the monitors in the sterile, white room beeped erratic rhythms. There was a moment, perhaps a second or two, so powerful I gave it a name: "The Turning." It was the moment I knew I could no longer hold onto him. It was the moment I understood everything in my being had to be focused on him, on his needs. And what he needed was to die. He was beyond medical help with leukemia, but it was the intensity of the bleed that flooded his brain that doused his passion for life. My job was quite simply to support him, to caress his hand, to touch his forehead while he faced his last task in life. My own needs blew away softly as though a gentle ocean breeze swept through the room.

* * *

Sitting in the kitchen, listening to Mother's labored breathing in the next room, I recognize "The Turning." It is not a knife

151

to the stomach, but an umbrella of peace and clarity, even simplicity, that can happen in an instant. Yet, somehow, through events that began days ago, I know Mother's passing is approaching.

The vision was the first sign. Two weeks ago, while my eyes rested and my mind was deep in meditation, her face appeared, suspended yet stable as though poised directly in front of me. Her features were delicate, but her expression was like a frightened child as she gasped, then struggled, to breathe in her last breath. My eyes flew open to block the power of the vision. My body jolted upright to break its spell, yet through the coming days, the vision sat in a hidden corner of my mind as if waiting, almost haunting my soul. I understood its meaning.

I watch Mother's caregivers, wondering if a mistake will be made, or if the night nurse, new to Mother's complex condition, will miscalculate a simple task. She does, but the errors are not enough to shake Mother's medical equilibrium, as tenuous as it is. An undissolved tablet causes coughing, but not serious choking. A reduction in fluids decreases her urine output, but does cause dehydration. The mistakes are minor.

Still, her urination ceases—the first sign of a urinary tract infection for my mother. The on-call hospice nurse catheterizes her to release the pressure. Her assigned hospice nurse, Jenni, another woman who wears white wings on her back, comes to the house. The details of our words etch deeply into my memory.

"You are right, Jeanette, she has a bladder infection." Jenni has been the lead on Mom's hospice team for the last year. We have treated Mom three times while on hospice, warding off different infections. Before, she at least had enough muscle control to smile, but now even swallowing saliva, a simple, unconscious muscular response, is as precarious as teetering on the edge of the Golden Gate Bridge. "I'll order some antibiotics."

"Jenni, wait. We need to talk about this."

"Okay." She pauses, waiting to hear me speak.

"Is it harder to die from a bladder infection when there is no sensation?" Mom had long lost her ability to feel pain in that area of her body. "Or is it harder to die from pneumonia?" I know it will be one or the other. It is how people in her condition die, unless the patient has a stroke or is lucky enough to have a fast cardiac arrest.

Jenni's searching eyes focus on me, her affect steady. Calmness surrounds her when she talks about death. She is gentle and direct. "It is probably easier to die from a bladder infection, Jeanette."

"What will it be like?"

"The infection will go beyond her bladder, into the blood stream, and…"

"And," I nod my head as I interrupt her, "Mom will develop septicemia and die from an infection in the bloodstream which overruns her organs."

"Yes. But we can keep her comfortable."

"Then, Jenni, I'm just not sure it is fair to treat her." She looks at me, her face trained not to show emotions, but to absorb emotion from the hearts of the many patients and family who need her support. "How long do we continue to prolong her life when it is at her expense? This can't be about me. About what I want. I'd keep her forever. It has to be about Mom. Her needs have to come first."

"You have the right to not treat, Jeanette."

"I keep thinking if it was me lying on that bed, and she was my daughter, I would be furious if she kept me alive yet one more time. Just furious."

Before Mother could at least smile, and parcel out her kisses. Now, muscle contractions not only stop her smile, but jeopardize her ability to swallow, and each choking episode sends terror through my body—not just hers.

"Jenni, I need to call my siblings. Go ahead and order the prescription. We should have it here, just in case."

"I can do that, Jeanette."

While my heart cracks, my composure, my exterior calm, matches that of the nurse who stands in front of me. "Are you okay with this, Jenni?"

She pauses, then with a softness in her voice says, "You have every right to stop treatment." She shifts her weight to her other foot. "I just wish I could have you speak to my other families."

I retreat upstairs to my bedroom, searching for a refuge to call the family. *What will I say to them? What words will soften the impact?* Puzzling over which sibling to call first, I pull up my oldest brother's number on my cell phone. Birth order becomes my guide, less about favoritism, and more reflective of a need for direction or perhaps some small pocket of certainty.

I repeat the scenario to each sibling. Each one's reply echoes the same sentiment, "Don't treat. It's time. She's suffered enough."

The decision to not treat feels like an avalanche tumbling toward me, knowing at some deep primordial level fate simply happens to us. Calm sets in. I complete daily tasks step-by-step, avoiding the fight within, wondering how soon I will lose her if I do not treat, whether or not she could rally if I did. She might rally for a few days, maybe weeks, but only to continue to decline into an increasingly difficult death. My angst leads me to the phone again. I call our physician. I want one more vote.

Dr. Bae answers his cell on the second ring. We have teamed on Mother's behalf for fourteen years, and even though he is not her hospice physician, he never quit the team.

"Dr. Bae, it's me, Jeanette."

"How are you doing?" Between my mother, my husband and my own diseases, I suspect Dr. Bae has asked me this question dozens of times.

"I'm hanging in." It seems the only phrase that is nondescript in a descriptive way. "It's Mom."

"What's going on?"

"Dr. Bae, she has another urinary tract infection." I pause, selecting my words with care, but Dr. Bae reads my fleeting silence as a sentence completed.

"Urinary tract? What makes you think it's an infection?"

"She can't urinate. The hospice team catheterized her, and the infection debris was very visible."

"Oh, I see. Okay." Dr. Bae hesitates, then adds, "Jeanette, this time we don't treat."

"That was my thought, too." I sigh with some relief these words came from his mouth before mine.

I hate the decision to not treat. I hate being responsible for decisions which surely should be owned by God. Yet, had it not been for my insistence on quality medical care, quality caregivers, diet, exercise, and on and on, Mother would have died some years ago. In some ways, I have already played the role of God—I do not like His job.

But buried in the decision to allow death is a kindness, a tenuous turmoil of love and concern. She is suffering now. She simply does not deserve to suffer.

The antibiotics arrive later that day. They sit on the kitchen counter—unopened. My life with Mother which began at my birth would soon end with her death.

Each day Mother declines. She never spikes a temperature from a bladder infection turned septicemia, but the residue in her urine is startling. She is hungry; yet swallowing is a task. Her esophageal muscles seem to fight her desire to eat, creating coughing and choking sensations. The caregiver thickens her food to a paste which sometimes causes more catching in her throat. Liquids are even more hazardous. Toothpaste is impossible as she has no ability to spit, so we are advised to dip her toothbrush in mouthwash. Today the toothbrush is too wet, and Mom sputters and coughs as the tiniest amount of fluid seeps into her bronchial tubes. I am haunted by the choking I witnessed in my vision.

She eats less. She drinks less. Then she quits.

Today, hospice begins round-the-clock nursing shifts. The nurse sits across the kitchen table from me as I provide her with Mother's complicated medical history. She takes notes, completes forms, and asks questions. She listens to me tell the stories of love, the charming, warm stories about a compassionate, intelligent woman. I have a million stories to tell about her, but I limit myself today. After a while, the nurse stands up, stethoscope in hand, and walks into the dining-room-turned-hospital-room to examine her patient.

In the silence of my kitchen, the familiar feeling comes to me, touches my heart, then fills my whole soul with a peace Webster, himself, would never be able to describe. "The Turning" is here. My fears, my needs, blow away like dry leaves. Everything is about Mother's needs now. And she needs to die.

My Mother, My Friend, My Child
December 2012

Her body lies still. The only visible movements are the swelling of her chest with each attempt to breathe, and the steady beat of her tough, little heart. She wears my long-sleeved grey pajama top, but we have put it on backwards; buttons meant for the front are unhooked in the back, the sleeves covering her arms. If we need to change her top, we can avoid hoisting her up and pulling it over her head. Every action we take must minimize her discomfort.

I cannot sit on the bed, nor lie next to her. When I try, the arthritis in my back screams little messages of pain up my spine. I rarely let it have the last word, so I ask the hospice nurse to help me move a chair, one I have rigged up with padding, a neck support, and a lower back pad. This chair is the only chair which allows me to lean back, meditate, sleep, and now to be with Mother through her death. I want to be here, by her side.

Mother's eyes open when she coughs and sputters, fervently inhaling molecules of air which must penetrate a thick, white paste at the back of her throat. She is dehydrated. She has not had anything to drink or eat for two days, I guess. Maybe three days, but the dark of night and the light of day blur together during a death watch. For all I know, the world stopped spinning, and put an end to the merry-go-round of life.

The hospice nurse is here as much for me as she is here for my mother. No one on the hospice team would allow us to be alone at Mom's death for while death is a solitary experience, it is best completed within a community. My siblings will not come, one sick with pneumonia, one with the flu, and one who finds it hard to think of a lasting memory of Mother withering away. He had the courage to say it. Surely, we all feel this way.

For me, Mother's dying is not about us. It is about her. Yet grief is like a fence limiting our views, often skewing our ability to understand what sits directly in front of us. I feel sad for Mother, but it reduces the human complexity of watching this death. The house is quiet, save for words spoken with caregivers, and one little woman trying to breathe.

Stethoscope around her neck, the nurse examines Mother again. She listens to her breathing, and checks her oxygen levels. After a while, she turns to me.

"Feel her hands. See how cool they are?" I nod my head. "Do you see how the skin on her feet and hands is becoming a bluish-purple color?"

"You mean the mottling?"

"Yes." The nurse pauses, then refocuses her eyes from her patient to me. "Jeanette, your mother is actively dying."

Actively dying. I write this new term on a pad of paper, the same pad I use to write out the grocery list. *Actively dying.* My mind toys with this new phrase, puzzled by it, perhaps a bit stunned, or maybe just detached. I do not want to understand this concept, this state of being called "actively dying," lest the full weight of its definition becomes real. I should throw the pad and the paper in the garbage, but for some reason I resist.

"It is possible your mother will die on my shift. If not, probably tomorrow morning's shift."

I go up to my room and go to bed. "*Breathe in, breathe out. Slow your thoughts, Jeanette. Stay focused.*" Finally, I drift into a light level of slumber, but wake in the middle of the night. Slipping partway down the stairs, I peer into the dining room to see the hospital bed. Mother has not moved. What did I expect? She would be sitting up and chatting with the hospice nurse? But expectations are not the same as hopes. I watch myself as I step in and out of the flowing emotions of grief. It helps to suspend judgment and simply observe myself. I go back to bed, yet wonder where the anger is, why it has not shown itself.

The next morning I slip down the carpeted stairs to tell her I love her. It seems the only comfort I can find is when I hold the now frail hand which held mine for so many years. The nurse notices a change in Mother when I enter the room.

"The sound of your voice seems to calm her. Your mother even responds to your voice when you are in another room." I decide I will stay by her side until she passes. It is a comfort I need as well.

There is a shift change this morning, too early for my liking. A new nurse comes in the front door, spends 15 minutes with the outgoing nurse, is quickly introduced to me, and the staff change is done. Over. Except it is not over. Fifteen minutes is not enough time to explain the complexities of Mother's medical history, so unknowingly the new nurse attempts to turn Mother on her side, allowing her good lung to fill with fluid while leaving her compromised lung gasping for air. I change Mother's position quickly, explaining my reasons while doing so. Each time I speak, the nurse listens more. Soon we establish why she needs my wisdom, and how much Mother and I need hers.

The new nurse chats as I recline beside my mother. Strange how conversation continues even while death approaches, but it does, sometimes giving a sense this day is a normal day. Yet for me, there is nothing normal about this day or any other day when someone I love so deeply is in the process of passing. And so I talk, quietly, close by, so my mother can hear me.

It has been four days now since my decision to not treat Mother's infection. The wisdom of my choice is pummeled by doubts as though pebbles flit through the air stinging my skin. *Was this the right time for her to die?* How does one know? All I really seem to comprehend is she trusted me to make her decisions. I love my mother. I hate this decision.

The Parkinson's contracts Mother's muscles and her arms become rigid. They hold like planks of boards in the air above her body. To lower these limbs would surely tear her muscles. The nurse talks about the pain she must feel, and encourages more liberal use of morphine. She is right. Comfort is our only goal now. I fill the syringe with another dose and slip it under her tongue, praying it will not cause her to choke.

A crack emerges in my self-induced calm as I watch this fading woman on the clumsy hospital bed. She begins to cough, no, it is a hacking that seems to rise from the deepest part of her lungs. It is the wretched paste which has collected in the back of her throat, so we try to siphon it out with a slender tube connected to a loud vacuum pump. We give her medications to help dry the secretions in her mouth. Before, it would clear her throat and allow her to breathe. Now, as her body dehydrates, the phlegm is too thick to siphon and the pump steals the air from her lungs. There is no win; just impending death.

The nurse evaluates Mother's condition, looks at me and says, "Your mother is actively dying." But she does not die. She coughs, sputters, and opens her tearing eyes when she cannot get enough air. Each time I see this, my brain sends waves of panic through my nervous system tensing every muscle, every fiber putting me on full alert. And yet she does not die.

What have I done? Why has breathing become such a pivotal issue? Why has the bladder infection been so quiet, so innocuous? Why is Mother ignoring she is actively dying?

We make a decision to give Mother larger doses of morphine. The medication buys her a few hours, then her breathing slips back into hacking and her eyes fly open showing her panic again. The more I watch, the more I wonder, *Did I make the right decision to not treat?*

The day slips into night. I never leave her side except to eat in the next room, and to exercise upstairs to relieve my pain. My chair is tilted back, allowing me to rest while holding her hand and peering into her face. I do not sleep, but my mind finds a quiet corner where I can stabilize my thoughts, allowing me to piece together my scant emotional reserves.

I cannot find the anger in my grief, but as Saturday dawns with new light, I find more questions, more doubts, more concerns. *Why is she holding on?*

The nurse wonders the same as she gently tends to Mother's needs. "Is she waiting to see someone?"

"She has three other children, but they won't be coming. Perhaps if I let her hear their voices by phone it will give her closure." I call each sibling to explain she appears to be holding on, letting each of them say their goodbyes while I hold the phone to her ear. It cannot be easy to suddenly formulate the last few words each would tell a mother who has given love so warmly, so without judgment.

My sister, ill with pneumonia, had two days with Mom not long ago, meeting both mother and daughter's needs. My younger brother, his heart always exposed, had visited Mother the most through the years. It is my older brother, the least likely to demonstrate emotion, whose well-being concerns me the most. Over the summer, her weak finger would point to pictures of him in old photo albums, pages made of black construction paper, tied together with string. Although smiling was difficult, she would find the words, "My Baby." He, too, has been ill, but had decided she did not remember him. Yet hearing the sound of his voice lifted her eyebrows when other muscles could no longer move. She responded the same to each of her children.

It has taken two days to fine tune the timing and the amount of morphine to buy her comfort. She sleeps more now. Her bladder releases less fluid, but her lungs loosen, seemingly gaining fluid. *It isn't supposed to be this way.* She was expected to have a temperature and gently fade into death, but she holds on. Her little heart keeps beating in a steady, methodical way. As my inner peace starts to slip away, I remind myself this is Mother's path. I am here to support her as she completes her last life task.

Another day dawns bringing two more shift changes since yesterday. Today's nurse reiterates what the first four said. "She is actively dying." This one also expects death will most likely happen on her shift. I cannot bear to leave Mother's side. My first husband died when I walked out of the bedroom for a few fleeting moments. A heart should never die alone.

Tonight Nurse Six arrives, another new face in an ongoing process, triggering another orientation and ongoing coaching. She, too, is special, clearly a pre-requisite for hospice nursing, but she is less settled in her job and her somewhat nervous chatter continues much of the night. When I try to meditate my way into calmness through the night, she asks me repeatedly, "Are you okay?"

I am unclear what she expects. Should I be weeping or wailing as Mother actively dies? Should I be agitated or angry? Each time, I answer calmly, "Yes, I am okay." Each time I know weeping, agitation and anger sit at my back door, death waiting to unleash each one. But this is Mother's journey. I have no time to grieve. For now, I sit holding her hand, transforming the emotions of grief into little whispers of love to this beautiful woman who lies before me. Nothing could be more important.

In the morning, my younger brother texts me. His wife wants to visit Mother, sealing the special bond that existed between them. My brother and his wife will bring two teenage daughters, and I fear, with them comes an energy which could upset this environment built around serenity, yet I welcome their visit.

My sister-in-law walks in the door, greets me with a quiet hug, then slips to the other side of the bed. She picks up Mother's hand and caresses it. Through the hours, it seems as though she never sets this small, swollen hand down, nor does she move from Mother's side. She glides into the mourning process like a ballerina moving through a soft cloud.

While the girls do not hold the hand of their dying grandmother, they follow their mother's lead of quiet respect and reverence. How grateful I am they sense the surroundings. How pleased I am for Mother these lovely women are in her presence. It is as if our hearts beat in the same rhythm, perhaps sing the same song.

My brother steps into the makeshift dining-turned-hospital room, and greets our mother. He is quieter than normal, but he speaks in greater volume than the women in the room. He lasts a few minutes, then gets up and moves to the kitchen. He empties my garbage, then walks back into Mom's room, and says a few words to her. He wisely paces his emotions by repeating the cycle several times finding a new way to help each time he leaves the room. This is hard on him, Mother's youngest child. It is hard to watch a loved one die, but we do not sit at her side for ourselves. We sit in her honor. She owns this process called dying; we simply love her through it.

Night falls and another nurse comes. Monday morning brings yet another nurse, but this is one I have met before, and I am grateful. I am tired of orienting a new person every twelve hours, of getting accustomed to a new personality twice a day, regardless of how nice these women are. I am spent. I do not need change at a time when I need every ounce of stability I can find. But it is my only irritation with this hospice service.

Mother's pulse still beats at a normal pace as though she were walking the hills in our neighborhood as she did four times a day for so many years. We can see the carotid on her neck pulsing with a surprising spirit, yet while her eyes tear, they do not open now. Her limbs lie quietly, but her chest continues to heave as she struggles for air. As I bring my face close to hers, I can hear the swishing of water as though a river runs through her lungs. A stethoscope is not required.

Suddenly, Mother coughs in her ongoing fight to bring air into her lungs. Her eyes, having been closed for two days, open briefly, with that look, the same fearful expression I saw in the vision, the same sense of anxiety in her brown eyes. It was the haunting look of a child being taken from its mother, and I know now I must completely release her. My mother, my friend, my child is truly actively dying.

I hold her hand near my heart, and ease close to her face whispering assurances she will be okay, that it will all be over soon. I tell her how much I love her once again. I assure her there will be other loved ones waiting for her, and I list them by name—her parents, my father, her aunts and uncles. I promise her son-in-law, Bob, will be there waiting to help her to the other side. I promise her I will be okay—the only promise of which I am not confident.

Her heart beats wildly as her carotid bounces and flails, then stops. Simply stops. She is no more. This woman that I hold in such high esteem, this child that I love so dearly, no longer fights for a breath.

I place my head on her chest, and I begin to cry.

The Quiet Between the Walls
January 2013

It is as if I can hear the house breathe. Each breath in brings the sounds of life past: the soft clatter of dishes in the sink; the whisper of my mother's voice; the clamor of my husband's favorite newscasters. Each inhale is a quiet cacophony of memories, reminders of the love and laughter that flowed from room to room. Now the house exhales. The kitchen, the dining room, the den, the living room, all four bedrooms are so very silent that I listen for a heartbeat. Each time I listen, I hear less. Each time I hear less, I try to hear more. It is not a battle I will win.

This house held our lives within its walls for ten years. Now it echoes back the sound of my husband's hands lightly slapping my butt as he walked by, grinning as he would exclaim, "Hey, Babe." He took pride in owning these two cheeks, confident once he touched them, all other hands were forbidden. Bob was right. He has been gone for two years, yet somehow, he still owns my "butt."

The kitchen is spacious now, just one person moving about. Before, there were caregivers who scurried around cleaning, cooking, and feeding Mother. Zena, Ailyn, Ruth, Pat, May and more, most from the Philippines, a "beautiful" country they would tell me, treated Mother with respect and dignity, honoring her as though she had traces of royalty. These women left family, often children, in hopes of being able to send money back home. Their sacrifice was our gain. I miss their voices, their singing, and the love they brought into our home. The house breathes with less depth in their absence.

I walk by my mother's room, and the quiet transforms into a rhythmic pulsing in my head. Her loss is the most recent, and the sight of her pink bedspread, her jewelry box sitting on her dresser, and the crystal bedside lamp owned by three generations now, makes my insides weak. I know I must clean out her room, but the container that holds her ashes still sits in the closet. My instinct is to throw the box against the wall, yet my need is to cradle what remains of her in my arms. Instead, I quickly shut her door. I do not like her being dead. I just want her home. I want both of them home—alive and in the flesh.

Yet they are home. I still feel their presence, but less so. Sometimes there are funny reminders, such as the television or the chandelier in the dining room. Both still have a way of turning on unannounced, but less frequently now. Cupboards close downstairs when no one is home but me. I can hear the noises in my office, and I sit and shake my head with a smile. I love this odd, playful support from, I assume, the other side.

But this house is built for four. I am one. The march of time pulls me forward as I form a new life. The hand is played; the deck is stacked. I must move on.

It's just a house, brick and mortar, Bob used to say. *Don't get attached*, he would tell me. It is easy to let go of run-of-the-mill brick and mortar, but how does one say goodbye to memories? To walls, adorned with our lives in pictures, walls that absorbed our laughter, our occasional fights, even our passion? How does one leave the kitchen where Mother, when confused, would call me Mommy?

But what puzzles me most is what I understand the least. How do I leave their spirits, or souls, or ghosts—or whatever phrase one might choose—that still give me comfort? When I walk out the front door for the last time, will they walk with me? I cannot endure any other thought.

And so, I search for closure. Closure to honor the memories I have collected, closure to celebrate the beauty we shared together. Enough closure to leave, but not enough to lose the presence of those I love.

I will cry when I hand the keys to the new owner. I will feel the pain when I walk down the steps, open my car door and drive away. Perhaps what I need is a celebration of sorts, a tribute to life after death, for that is what I face now: my life after their death. Shall I honor my next home in some special way to help me let go of the home we all shared? Maybe. But if I do, there is one invitation that will be shared in the quiet spaces between the walls.

"Mom, Bob, join me. Please."

Crosses
March 2013

My Love,

There is so much yet to learn of each of us, but what excitement the future holds.

Robert Canady, May 20, 1995

"Jeanette's just lonely."

My words stuck inside my throat as I tried to respond to her comment. A few phrases finally passed through my lips, although the few that did were surely nonsensical. *Lonely?* If I had been drinking water, it would have sprayed into the next town.

Mary linked my name to the word lonely. Out loud. She did not direct the comment to me. She directed it to the other members of our writers group, all in deep discussion of my recently written chapter on losing a spouse. There was no trace of unkindness in her voice. Mary is witty, edgy, and at times humorously acidic, but below her breast rests the heart of a saint. It was Mary who cooked a whole week's worth of food when Bob was dying; it was Mary who took a day off work to surprise me and drive me to the hospital for a procedure; it is Mary who texts me on a regular basis to see if I am up for a movie.

And it is Mary who sees through my loneliness—apparently before I do. *Lonely?* Until she put the word in my vocabulary, I had effectively avoided it as though never uttering the six letters would ward off loneliness like a cross defending a soul against Dracula. Now, I can almost feel the teeth on my neck.

When my first husband died, I did not start the grief process with loneliness. The process began with being alone in a unique way, like a state of being in-between, a state of connectedness. It was as if Jack sat in the same kitchen, walked down the same hall, stood in the same family room. I was not lonely. One might say I savored this private time with my deceased husband.

I would hear footsteps on the stairs, one step at a time. Unbelieving, I called a handyman to fix my squeaking steps explaining that the sun streaming through the skylight above was heating the stairs causing them to creak as though someone were walking on them. He controlled his grin, then calmly explained the steps would not creak from the sunlight. They would creak only if someone walked on them, he explained, then he put his shoe on a step, gave it his full weight, and we listened as the stair groaned under the burden of his body. As his words and actions calmly assaulted my logic, my emotions danced. How could I be lonely? It seemed Jack was still there.

When Bob, my second husband, died, there was a funeral to arrange, celebrations of his life to create, and financial details to organize. Even before the calmness set in, odd little events began to occur. Electronic devices seemingly had wills of their own, like the TV turning on at will in the middle of the night. My ailing mother knew of Bob's passing before anyone told her. Each event soothed me, as though spirits, souls or perhaps ghosts left a door open just slightly, just enough to allow some comforting contact. A psychiatrist would describe this as a grief reaction. A minister would describe it as a sign from God. A grief counselor would say they hear about these events frequently. I did not attempt to classify these events. I was simply grateful for having had them.

But this desire to be "alone" with the departed came with an odd disorientation, a turning upside down of my life. I called it the "Walking Fog." It was as though I had stumbled out onto the wing of a plane in flight, and tried to walk through the clouds only to find my sight was hazy, my thoughts confused, my words slow. With my first husband's death, even my voice changed. It had so little energy, projecting was impossible. My already deep voice became deeper until even answering machines could not record my attempts to speak, repeatedly cutting me off midsentence. As hard as I tried to be heard, it seemed I did not exist.

The "Walking Fog" served a purpose: it protected me from the onslaught of emotions hiding around the corner I was about to turn. The Fog softens the shock of loss, allowing it to seep into life at a slower pace, a pace the mind can survive and the heart can tolerate. As the Fog lifts, the pain descends. As the pain descends, being alone transforms into loneliness, revealing a powerful sense a loved one is drifting away. Reality really does suck.

Lonely? I guess so, but loneliness is an emotion, a fleeting experience like anger and fear. They all bite with sharp teeth, and at times swirl me into a downward spiral like a tornado in reverse. It is hard to reach out when the dust of grief gets too thick, so I act before the winds blow too hard.

I ward off loneliness with my crosses: my friends, my love of learning, and the sense of purpose writing instills in me. Before Bob died, planning free time was insignificant, consisting of short, rapid requests, "Bob, let's go to a movie today." That simple, that short. Now, I make sure my time is scheduled in advance as I attempt to fill the holes that loss left in my life.

Jeanette's just lonely? Damn it. I have not contacted a single friend yet. And my calendar is empty for the next five days. I search for my phone, pick it up, and begin to text.

Mary, want to see a movie this weekend?

Sea of Stuff
April 2013

There are times when this house feels so big, all 2,715 square feet of it, as I wander from room to room. If I speak aloud, the walls would surely bounce echoes to and fro. But you see, I do not speak aloud as there is no one to listen save an occasional spider, and I do not know how to *speak* spider. So I wait impatiently for a childhood friend to return my call. One day stretches into two, then four, then six.

Why hasn't she called? She texts, "I'm beat again today. Can you talk tomorrow night?" Each evening I listen for my phone to ring, resisting the temptation to call other friends in hopes of hearing from her. But my phone does not cry out to me. It doesn't even whimper. Instead, I sit in my abundantly quiet house, and percolate my frustration like a stale pot of strong coffee. Today it seems life is all about me.

It is hard for many friends to understand my loss not having experienced it themselves. I miss my husband. I miss my mother. I even miss her caregivers. Life was full of caring for and caring about, but my care targets passed away. They just died, they expired or whatever hellish word one might use. Now, too much of my day is spent avoiding the last tasks of loss: the tossing or giving away of their personal items. Each T-shirt has his slightly musky odor. Each blouse reminds me of her smile.

It seems as if all I touch is a piece of life lost. His desk drawer is full of his hand-written notes to himself. Her little shoes with their deeply worn soles, soles which used to take her up and down the hills of our neighborhood several times a day, still cover the floor of her closet. Sometimes, I peer inside her empty bedroom—why I am not sure—and I am quickly reminded it is easier to keep her door closed.

Yet strange as it seems, this house comforts me. I suspect I feel Mom and Bob's presence, their support. Yet the lack of human voices can drain a soul in a way that causes one to wonder if the ear drum is the sole source of incoming human data. God forbid I should lose my hearing even if there is nothing to hear.

I know I must descend once again into the pit of hell called a garage. Bob's stuff, Mom's stuff, my grandparent's stuff—most of it is still there, and much of it is strewn, I would say, over most of the cement floor. There are spots on which I can hop through the sea of stuff, but much of the gray concrete is blanketed by assorted items giving the appearance of a floating landfill. I feel as if I am drowning.

When my first husband died, it took two years for the waves of emotion to ease each time I ventured into his meticulous garage with floor-to-ceiling built-in storage cabinets. I would scurry from the house to my car, eyes focused on my car door so I could avoid glancing at his racing bicycles neatly hanging from the ceiling. I finally managed a garage sale, selling some things, and giving away what I could not sell.

Since the passing of my second husband, it is the organizing, the pricing, the advertising, the bartering, the saying goodbye to each tool, each implement, each memory that pushes me into a state of overwhelm as if falling off the tallest of bridges.

For months I have growled beneath my breath, *How the hell do I sell all this stuff?* Do I try ads in the local paper, or online, or on Facebook? The ads would bring people, mostly men, to the house to rummage through tools and hedge trimmers and assorted garage type implements. My neighbor, a young, tall man, offered to be at the house if unknown types wanted to come by. But the challenge was also in writing the ads.

FOR SALE
Long metal thing with a hole in the top
Price unknown

I have needed solutions, but grieving and stress have narrowed my ability to see, like a horse wearing blinders walking down an empty road. I can sense obvious solutions, the "there-is-only-one-way-to-do-this" type, but I have no vision beyond simplistic, unimaginative fixes. Then last week, the clouds in my mind lifted just enough to allow a creative breakthrough.

Trees close to my home needed to be cleared for fire safety, yet the cost reached far beyond my budget. While negotiating price, I remembered my overflowing garage housed a fire-truck-red, chest-high tool cabinet waiting for a new home. The gardener reduced his price, and the trade was made. His smile matched mine.

The next day, I started giving items away. My mother's commode, walker, and mattress found a home with a woman just released from the hospital. My heart danced a tiny pirouette, and the rush from that one act of kindness lasted for hours.

Encouraged, I called girlfriends and invited them to come visit my garage floor. Wendy needed tools for her new farm, so she worked on my sprinklers in trade. Sherri wanted tools for her partner. Pam exclaimed, "Don't give away anything 'til I see what you've got. I love tools!"

I must have sighed with relief each time someone needed an electric drill. I had seven of them. Seven. Two husbands, seven electric drills. I had almost forty of those long, metal things with the holes in the top in dozens of sizes, most likely gear wrenches from my Internet search. Most of them, along with three drills, have new owners now, and I can see a greater patch of the cement floor. While it somehow helps to know these tools live on in the hands of others, it was the smiles of friends and gardeners as they put yet another treasured tool into their cars that bounced my spirits a bit closer to the sky.

Clothing was the toughest. Or at least that is what I expected when it came time to donate Bob's wardrobe. His dapper suits, striking ties and white, crisp shirts would go to a charity which provided clothes for the jobless for interviews. His casual clothes were to be given to Wounded Warriors. Yet, none of this seemed to lessen the pain as his suits still carried the faint smell of his Old Spice aftershave. When the gravity of grief held my feet to the floor, I called a friend, a former neighbor who used to work for me running my office. She could organize better than bees in a hive. I asked for help. I had to. I could not face the touch of his clothes alone.

She thought she would help me organize, but she did so much more. She came to the house, sat at my kitchen table and said, "Before we start, I have something to share with you." She smiled a smile that wavered as her eyes misted slightly. As steadfastly as possible, she continued, "Jeanette, I've just been diagnosed with Alzheimer's." I understood the power of her words, in some ways perhaps more than she, having cared for my mother for so many years. As I watched the tears slip down her cheeks, all my fear, my dread, my worries of sorting through old clothes evaporated faster than a drop of water on a scalding pan.

There was but one thought in my mind. *I must do everything I can to make this the best possible experience for my friend.* For the next four days we laughed, and organized, and carted clothes from here to there. We spoke from the heart when we needed to, and giggled whenever we could. Her gift to me was immeasurable: she allowed me to give to her. She reminded me life extends far beyond my world without ever speaking the words.

I doubt she ever knew how much she helped me heal during her visit.

Tonight I sit, once again, in a quiet house save the whirring of the air conditioner. My garage still calls to me like a bearish apparition sporting a 666 stamped on its forehead. Once again, I wait for my friend's call. She has been one of my closest friends since we were eleven years old. *Why hasn't she called yet? What could possibly be going on?* I stop as it hits me. My friend is a social worker who helps mentally ill homeless people find shelter. She cares for a family member with a mental disorder. She has a young, mentally ill nephew sitting in jail waiting to be sentenced. She is a mother and a wife. She cooks, she cleans, she pays bills.

Why doesn't she call me? *Life is not all about you, Jeanette.*

The Power of Rabbits
May 2013

The tears slipped down my cheeks as I held the bunny, one hand holding its tiny bottom and cotton puff tail, the other wrapping around the rabbit's tummy, while his paws folded over the back of my hand. I tried to give him a sense of security as I lifted him eye level, which must seem like the height of a giant to a bunny that could fit into a medium-sized bowl.

In the haze of my dream, the bunny's wet, little nose and damp eyes were a sign. The bunny had influenza, deadly for a rabbit within 48 hours. His eyes spoke to me, preparing me, for he knew he was going to die.

It might have been the tears on my face that woke me from the dream, but the ache building in my heart had more power.

* * *

When the gardener had come to clear the dead brush off the hill in my backyard, my instructions were clear, "Don't clear out the undergrowth by that tree. That's where the rabbit lives. He will leave if you do, and I don't want his home disturbed." But my instructions were unheeded, unheard, apparently unremarkable. When I stepped outside to inspect their completed task, the bunny's home was gone, not a branch nor a leaf left. Not a pine cone or a pine needle remained. The gardener had done a remarkable job.

But there was no trace of the little rabbit that lived in my yard. The grinding motors of saws and leaf blowers must have seemed to him like an explosion at a neighbor's home would seem to us.

One more loss. One less little soul to protect.

This was the bunny Bob had come to know before he died. We would watch the rabbit outside our kitchen window, cavorting with another with exceptionally long ears. Bob could always tell them apart, observant as he was. Mother knew the bunnies, too. She would sit, speechless from her Parkinson's, occasionally able to smile when one would spring straight off the ground, flip his little butt in the air, and do a 180 degree turn. I can't remember the name we gave him, but I suspect the one with long ears was killed by a coyote as he disappeared one day some time ago.

After Bob died and Mother passed, after the caregivers and hospice team moved on, there was just me and one bunny living alone on this property. The air was as still as a lake without a hint of a ripple. Caring for others had become my purpose, the meaning in life, and suddenly, at Mother's last breath, my purpose had no target save one little rabbit. Listening to my own breath was exhausting.

Seems as though I should have been able to protect this little creature. Perhaps my mother and my husband as well, and while I cannot seem to stop Death, I have become her student. I have learned, through the tears of loss, sadness happens … deep resounding sadness. Then it evaporates, giving way to the memory of Bob's smile, or a funny comment once made by my witty mother. At night when I crawl into my queen size bed, perfect for two bodies but oversized for one, once again the grief clogs up my heart until the tears clear it out.

I have found grief can bring a barren loneliness to my soul. Few can understand its wallop unless they have taken the punch. Having lost two husbands, I find I do not "heal" after losing a spouse. But with time, I feel less sting at the sight of my husband's old wallet, or a pair of my mother's shoes sitting on the floor of her closet, waiting for her small feet to slip inside. Most people do not realize the subtle sorrows hiding in my heart, yet the heart is where I keep the treasures of lives passed. The heart is the real home, not the house we live in.

Death taught me happiness is like a bird which lights briefly, then, at the slightest provocation, spreads its wings taking feathers to the wind. Happiness is found in time spent with friends and family; the fun of a new car; the excitement of a vacation. It is transient, for it comes and goes in the flash of a present moment.

But sadness shares this transience as well. Grief is to be respected, so I do not avoid its sadness. I give it the time it needs, no more, no less. I cry when my heart needs to cry. But I no longer search for happiness, either. Instead, I invite happiness by scheduling times that bring joy and laughter to my heart. I schedule slumber parties of girl-talk and movies and smiles with my delightful nieces, Allyson and Megan, or go on photo shoots with friends, or take classes. Sadness is seductive, so I have learned from Death I must balance tears with smiles.

People in my life are like air to my lungs. My house, in all its quiet, fails to converse with me, and the bunny only speaks to me in my dreams. Unchallenged by dialogue within these walls, my facile way with words rusts like an empty tin can, so I call friends, I Skype, I meet people for lunches and movies. After being alone—totally alone—for four or five days, it takes at least two hours of conversation to re-learn how to fluidly converse. At first, it seems as though my words are setting in my hand like a handful of pennies, each one dropping, slipping down an open drain as I try to grab them. Finally, my words flow once again proving to me how critical my social connections are. Another lesson from the teacher, Death.

And then there is the dreaded boredom. My mind, unchallenged, hosts all types of chatter—most of which is a clear departure from the ethics that guide my life. The chatter is petty, meaningless, and leads to mind-wandering escapades into the "anyone-whoever-did-me-wrong" path of thought. More complex than the simple lament of a country boy's loss of his truck, his gal and his dog, my brain hoards boredom chatter until it floods my soul, hurts my heart, and causes me to question friends and loved ones. It creates space for the tempting power of angst, leaving me to wonder what words I may have failed to say to my dear husband before he died, what symptom I might have missed as my mother declined, or what I could have done to save the last little bunny. A bored mind is not a good one.

Such chatter leaves little room for quality thinking and positive thoughts, so Death taught me to search for distractions. I soon learned distractions come in many variations, from swatting an annoying fly, to a simple movie, or even a passion. I found my passion. I need to create. I want to play with words like a dancer plays with movement extending her arms to reach the hearts of her audience. I want to toy with rhythm in a sentence like a drummer beats his drum in search of a crescendo. I want—no, I need—the rush of endorphins from finishing a chapter, or a story, or even a Christmas letter. I must create. It is my way of surviving loss. It is my way of surviving life.

Yet while my efforts—socializing, learning, and creating—do me well, they are still paths to happiness as impermanent as a snowflake when the clouds fade, or a bunny's home after the brush is cleared. I need more. I have cared for a loved one or lived with someone who was dying for most of the last 22 years. The times were rich with meaning. As my heart ached, my soul grew, my compassion grew, my ability to love grew. I had purpose, and life had meaning. It was all in the giving.

And so I give support to friends and family as they face the painful hazards of life. I watch after bunnies that have lost their homes. And I write about the tough stuff in life, in hopes my experiences, my beliefs, will somehow touch others and lessen their pain. My reward has more power than a transient sense of happiness. As I pursue the meaning in my life, I find my purpose, a purpose which links me to the past and pulls me into the future. No, I will not cheat Death. But I will learn her lessons.

My mind is full of big thoughts as I sit in a house filled with silence save the rustling of my newspaper. Through my kitchen window, I peer at the pine trees in my backyard and the well-trimmed shrubs on the hill when a movement catches my eye. I see the flash of a white tuft of tail ducking into a thicket to my right. I hear a slight rustling of leaves to my left. Moments later, two bunnies are frolicking on my small patch of grass, one with very large ears. I smile. My bunny has come home. And he brought his long-eared, long lost friend.

Come Back
June 2013

My Love,
You have encouraged me in an important way,
With our conversation and love letter today;
As I drift into dreamland tonight
I shall hold you close til I get it right.
I love you more than a thousand ways,
You will experience that in the coming days.
So I will seal this letter with a kiss,
And hold tightly my memories of you, my bliss.

Robert Canady, May 20, 1995

There are days when I can feel his breath warming the back of my neck. My body tingles with anticipation as I lean my head to the side exposing this delicate spot. I stand still for that moment, and wait for the soft touch of his lips upon my skin, the strength of his arms to enfold me. I feel his body wrapping around me, protecting me from the world. I melt into his sensuous self, and I am safe. It is as if he were still alive.

Something always breaks the magic: the voice of a child playing in the neighbor's yard, the tone of my cell phone ringing in the other room, or the television blurting out some meaningless commercial. Reality sucks.

On May 18th, it will be two years since my husband died. It has taken me two years to say the word "died." I substituted "he died" with "he passed," as though terminology would make the outcome less final. "Dead" is in-the-ground, over. "Passed" felt more respectful somehow, but more importantly, it felt more alive as if he had simply passed by the house and would be returning home.

I am not sure he has not. How else can I explain the television turning on to his favorite channel in the middle of the night, blaring at the level he required for his compromised hearing? How else do I explain lights going off and on? How else do I explain his breath on the nape of my neck? I understand the concept of magical thinking, but how does one explain magical thinking with physical evidence?

To me, Bob passed into another plane of existence, a place where he can send wisdom and love, and perhaps tweak a television. I worry not about what others think of these unusual events. I focus on the comfort they give me. And so, I talk to him—aloud—about anything.

"Bob, you would have laughed so hard watching Betty White's new show!" I blurted out just last night. I continued this conversation in the quiet of my thoughts.

Oh, you can see the show, can't you? I looked over to his easy chair. It was empty. It has been since the day he left for that last hospital trip, yet my eyes still searched the chair, looking for feelings of comfort more than tangible evidence of his presence.

Even if I am reluctant, time moves forward.

God, give him back! It was not Bob's fault he died, so I direct my anger at God. *Give him back to me!* This is not a request. It is a demand. I imagine myself a two-year-old, hitting and kicking my hardest, aiming my efforts at this Almighty Being while he, his hand on my forehead, calmly holds me at arm's length watching my tantrum. It just pisses me off, and increases my anger. This is getting nowhere, so I speak to Bob in quiet tones.

I don't want to move on, Bob! Why do I have to?
The response was so simple, so honest.

"You're there, and I'm here."

The future feels so different than the past.

A Letter to my Husband
March 2014

My Love,

You have been gone for almost three years now. Yet not a day goes by I do not think of you. I feel your presence, but less so, as though each day a piece of your soul slips deeper into heaven, or wherever energy goes once unleashed from a body. It is not where you are going that causes me discomfort. It is the slipping away, the loud quiet of your absence that puts an ache in my heart.

Yet, I know it is time.

I am over the anger. Once, I raised my voice and declared, How dare you leave me! I held on—pictures of you in every room in the house. I even selected a picture of you for the wallpaper on my cell phone. Shortly after you died, I threw the phone on the bed. When your smiling picture looked back at me, the pixels began to fade as though half of your face was disappearing. Soon the screen on my phone turned a deep black as if peering into an unending crater. It never recovered, much like you. It was as if you were telling me to take another step forward, another step away from you. A small piece of me, hiding in some corner of my body, wanted to slap you for dying. But even anger has a purpose. It insulated my soul from the profound pain of loss. Anger is easier than grief. But it carries too much guilt.

It was a pairing of two people who fit, you and me. Remember how it started? A shared intellectual curiosity, the first of many aphrodisiacs, I would say. Then we learned to play—me a constant target of your soft, flirtatious wit, a wit that, had I not respected you so completely, would have caused me to hide. Instead, you became a constant target of my desire, the depth of which can only spring from complete love, complete trust.

But even the best of fits are not perfect. Like most busy people, we allowed ourselves to slowly shift our mental focus to the dullness of daily chores. I did not notice that, over time, we kissed less frequently. Did you? We made love less. We quit holding hands in the movies. We quit being teenagers in love. I was the busier of the two of us, running a small business, caring for Mother. My heart aches when I wonder if you felt hurt. Such are the moments lost in time, I guess.

If you were here now, I would laugh with twinkling eyes. I would kiss your lips each time you entered a room. I would ask you to dance to a romantic song. I would sit on your lap and slide my hand up your leg just to see your dimples deepen. I would make love with you all night.

I would not forget relationships must be fed like flowers in need of rain. I would remember to tell you how much I appreciate you, to notice the simple things you would do for me each day. I would savor your kindness, your loyalty. I would savor the smell of your body, the taste of your lips. I would notice the mystery of love.

When you were alive, each time you held me in your strong arms the fears, the anxiety, the very pain of life evaporated. Poof! It was like magic. For months and months after you died, I felt your breath on the back of my neck, your chest behind me, your arms encircling me. Each day you left me with more strength. Over time, I could almost hear you whisper, "I'll hold you up until you can move forward." Those whispers got me through neck surgery, Mom's illness, her death, and finally—when the house had no breath but my own—the grief of losing you.

I still fancy myself a student of love. I suspect you agree. I have learned once someone I love is gone, each disregarded moment vanishes like ashes drifting on a wind. As you said so many times, "There are no do-overs in life, Jeanelle."

I have no do-overs left with you, but I am better for what I have learned. When I love again, I will laugh effortlessly. I will hold his hand walking on a beach. I will repay his kindnesses with kisses. I will fight with fairness. I will romance him until he tires. I will love with consistency rather than urgency.

For me, love is the fabric of life. It is a purpose. It is a symphony of voices as though each soul we have ever loved sings to us from far beyond. I hope you are pleased with what I have learned. You have sustained me well as though physical death is less real, less concrete than we seem to believe.

Still, you are with me less at this point in time. I can feel it. You can see my legs are not as wobbly from the impact of your death. I am taller, my face closer to God. I am braver, even as you slip away into the quiet.

But before you go, before you immerse yourself in the heavens, I must thank you. Thank you for the many whispers of encouragement. For wrapping me in your arms. For teaching me about love.

Now, I say to you what you told me before you died. I will see you on the other side.

Until then. All my love,

Jeanette

A Letter to my Readers:
Getting Through Grief

Dear Reader:

   Thank you for joining me on this challenging and sometimes painful path, a path full of awe and love for two remarkable people. By reading my book, you have experienced my journey through grief. You also saw me find my way back to a rewarding life. Now, I would like to show you the process I share with people to help them walk through their own grief.

   To start, I believe when we experience grief there are some truths. These truths will help us get through the process.

   One, grief is messy. A number of emotions may appear—sometimes out of nowhere and when least expected. While one person may experience anger with a departed loved one, another griever may not. Until Bob died, I never experienced anger with anyone I lost. I knew the cancer would take him, and I hurt for him as he faced it. I simply did not want him to leave me. With time the anger dissipated.

   Two, to manage the tough side of grief, we must be able to find our smile. After my first husband died, a dear friend gave me some advice. "You know, Jeanette," Gene said, "I read that when someone is living through grief, it's important to have things to look forward to." It was a simple statement, yet 23 years later I can still hear his words. He was so right. Gene's advice was a source of encouragement, so I planned social time to enjoy my friends. I felt encouraged to write. And as you know, I traveled to Africa for the experience of a lifetime. I cried off and on all the way through Kenya and Tanzania, but the endorphins the trip created helped carry me through the pain of loss.

Three, we do not all experience grief in the same manner. After watching two friends lose their spouses, it was apparent the way they managed loss was different than how I managed it. I needed to take a deep breath and live with the loss. Both my friends took short respites from life, but then both began dating to replace their loss. They were comfortable addressing the loneliness. I was comfortable being alone. The differences have nothing to do with what is right or wrong, but they demonstrate different responses. Each relationship is unique, and grief responses, in part, reflect the uniqueness of the relationship.

Four, when we grieve most of us do not fall apart. Many of us must get back to our responsibilities, so we do. When my second husband died, I still had to take care of my mother as she was dying. She deserved the same love and attention I had given Bob. In his book, *The Other Side of Sadness,* Dr. George Bonanno, describes this as resilience, and found that some 50-60% of us who experience grief adjust quite quickly despite typical day-to-day fluctuations. Dr. Bonanno believes if you think you are doing well, then you probably are. Crying, laughing and even a sense of wonder are all a part of healing. But they do not just come to us—minus the tears which seem to find us wherever we are. We must plan for joyous times to balance the painful ones. We must help ourselves through our own pain. And we must fulfill our purpose.

All of us respond differently through the grieving process, but part of grieving successfully is about personal decision making. Initially, putting one foot in front of the other was my way of moving forward. Eventually, writing helped me work through some of my loss, but more importantly, allowed me to create and I soon fell in love with writing. Whatever anchors you to life, be it children, grandchildren, your career, your volunteer work, or your religion, connect with those anchors. Your anchors reflect what is meaningful to you, and a life with meaning is what helps us heal in the grieving process. It is my hope the process I have outlined below will help you calm the grief residing in your heart.

Questions For Discussion
And Self Reflection

If you are going through grief or have experienced loss before, you might find it helpful to answer these questions for yourself. Let's look at my responses as an illustration of the process.

How did I respond before, during and shortly after my loss? What was this like for me?

I experienced a lack of clarity. No one really talks about the "walking fog" as I call it. Shortly before or after a loved one's loss, for many of us, our world becomes cloudy. It is hard to plan, hard to complete a list of tasks, and hard to remember much of anything. Emotions are so powerful, we can become numb.

Perhaps the best way to imagine the walking fog is looking out a plane's window when flying through a cloud. You cannot see in front of you, behind you, or to the sides. Now, imagine walking into a cloud only to realize your loss has dramatically changed your life, and your future is not clear. This can be very unnerving for many of us.

Sometimes, it is impossible to know how life will change. Even if much in our lives continues, such as an ongoing career, for most of us the loss of a key person leaves an amazing hole in our lives. The fog helps numb that pain. I believe it is the brain's way of protecting us from a significant emotional impact. My fog felt safe. The full impact of the pain could not descend.

I found grief responses are different from one loss to another. Each response to grief can be very different. My response to Jack's death was intense. The relationship had serious trust issues. The lack of financial planning added to the difficulty. Plus, I had no idea how manage my grief. I felt my world, as I knew it, die with Jack's last breath.

When Bob, my second husband, died, I had a personal understanding of grief which enabled me to help myself through the process. Plus, the relationships were very different. Bob was my soul mate, and I trusted him. For me, a lack of trust brings old hurts and wounds into the grief process, an already muddy process to experience.

When Mother died, she had experienced so much pain the last few months of her life I grieved the entire last year. I had not realized bringing my mother back home to die would basically stop my grieving for Bob. After her death, I spent little time mourning her, but immediately returned to grieving for Bob.

Did my response to grief change with time?

Yes, for me grief changes with time. It was about six months after the loss of my first husband that the intensity of grief, along with the walking fog, began to lift. By that time, I was falling in love with Bob, but the grieving process continued. As I wrote in the book, it seemed inconceivable to me I could be mourning the loss of one man while falling in love with another, yet I was. My time with Bob lifted my spirits, but in his absence I returned to mourn the loss of Jack. Having positive things, even falling in love, does not stop grief. It does, however, provide a balance in life as we work through our loss.

What did I need to help me get through this phase? How did I get what I need?

I needed help and I had to learn to ask for it. My learning task was to identify and communicate my needs to others, be it a tough conversation about anger, or the frightening task of asking for help. People often do not know how to help others facing loss. They often do not know what to say, and they do not know what we need. If we do not help them understand what we are facing, they will not be able to support us.

While Jack was dying, I was building a consulting business and helping him through his illness. One day, a friend who was carefully listening to me, noticed I failed to talk about any kind of support.

She looked at me and said, "Jeanette, do you have any help?"

I had to think about it, but it did not take long. My response was, "No." I had been so independent in my life I had not even noticed.

My friend looked at me, eyebrows furrowed across her forehead and she shook her head back and forth. She said, "You need to ask for help. And when you think you have enough, you need to ask again."

I asked, then I asked again and again until I could get Jack through the end of his life. I asked a friend to move in with us to take care of me and the house so I could focus on Jack. When my friend left for Christmas, I found myself alone with Jack. Concerned he might die, I called one of his professors with whom he had become close.

"Justin, would you come and sit with us? I want Jack to be able to die at home, but I don't want to be alone if he dies. Another friend is coming later, but I have no coverage for this afternoon."

I set the phone on its cradle, got up to unlock the front door, then promptly fell asleep on the bed next to my husband. When I awoke, Justin was napping in the easy chair in the corner of our bedroom. I had not heard when he tapped at the door, so he let himself in, and decided not to wake us. His kindness will forever be stored in my memory, not to mention my heart.

Our dear friend, Dean, did the same. He left a family dinner two days before Christmas to spend the night in that same easy chair in our bedroom. There was no way I could have been alone. The pain of losing someone is hard enough. Doing it alone: unbearable. Death is truly a community event.

So let people who genuinely care know how they can support you. And if friends say something in hopes of being supportive, yet their words seem unkind, try to remember they may not have experienced loss. (One of the classic comments is, "You must be so relieved it is over!") If they are good friends, give them the benefit of the doubt, and do what you can to keep your friends close. Even if they do not understand loss, they can help you maintain balance. Have dinner, see a movie, and laugh whenever you can.

What did I learn during this time?

To be clear about my motives. It is not always easy to recognize, but we do try to manage outcomes. The truth is we can fight to get our loved ones the best medical care possible in hopes of lengthening their lives. We can work to improve the quality of time they have left, and both are worth pursuing. However, we cannot control the destiny of others, regardless of how much we love them. Accepting that death is inevitable for all of us is not always easy, most notably when it is someone we love.

In my experience when a loved one is failing, we instinctively want to do everything we can to keep them alive. The question becomes, *are we keeping the patient alive for us?* The second question is, *are we keeping them alive at their expense?* I can't keep a loved one alive when pain and discomfort is at their expense.

To operate from my core values. I remember a day when Jack lay in the hospital. It was the day after a frightening hemorrhage. I was at home. I knew I needed to get out of bed, drive to the hospital to support Jack, but depression had stolen my soul that day. I cared about my husband, but was withering under his anger. It was so difficult at times, I had decided to rent a room locally so I could be there when he needed me, yet escape his moods. At the time, he was fairly stable and still working—until the hemorrhage.

I stared at the ceiling unable to get out of bed. I called a friend to ask if she could come and sit with me. Her response? "Oh sorry, I can't. I have to go grocery shopping."

I lay there so stunned. Finally, I looked up at the ceiling and began a conversation with God, something I do more frequently during difficult times. I said aloud, "God, what must I do now that I will be proud of at the end of my life?"

The answer was instantaneous. I rose from the bed, dressed and drove to the hospital. My learning was to do what is morally right. Staying with my husband and caring for him through his passing was the only option for me. When I do what is right, I have fewer regrets looking back.

To diffuse anger. During times of loss, sometimes what we value becomes very clear. That was the case for me. When my first husband was dying, my greatest desire was to help him calm his anger about his impending death. He was older, but was an athlete, a vegetarian and he fully expected to live many more years. Frustrated by his impending death, he focused his anger on me.

I remember one day he was incredibly angry. I looked at him and said, "I'm so tired of dealing with your anger. What is it you want from me?" It was the perfect comment to make.

He looked at me, stretched his arms toward me and said, "I just want you."

I looked at him, sitting on the bed like a small boy who had been scolded. "You just want me? That's all I need to know." I hugged him and said, "You've got me." His anger dissipated. Over the last three months of his life, it was as if we fell in love again.

To talk about love. Perhaps one of the most important gifts of all was the realization I must talk about love. When Bob was dying, I told him everything I loved about him: his kindness, compassion, intelligence. I told him how much I appreciated the love he showed my mother. What I got in return were words of love I will never forget: "I just wish I had 20 more years with you, Jeanette." These words touched my heart in ways I could not have predicted.

I did not discuss old fights or old issues. There were a couple I would have liked to lay to rest, but Bob had already apologized and it was up to me to release that angst. I have heard war stories from hospice workers about adults throwing items at each other across the bed of their dying mother, the result of old issues and terribly ineffective family cultures. I would have physically ejected anyone who tried to do that with either of my two husbands or my mother. People have the right to die in peace.

To listen to the dying. Bob spoke openly and with great grace about letting go of life. I listened to his words intently, and wish now I had taped his wisdom.

Hearing Jack was difficult. I had to listen carefully to what was *not* being said. He had fears about dying—unspoken fears. He needed to be understood even if he was unable to process all that was happening to him. He had the right to be heard, so I did my best to listen.

To understand dying is not about you: Most people prefer not to die alone, yet some people find it difficult to visit the dying. It does confront our greatest fears as we watch people actively dying. But for those who will not visit a loved one to say goodbye, I ask you this, how would you feel if your son or daughter or sibling refused to see you so you could say goodbye? Would you want your mother or father to die feeling unloved? Unappreciated?

If not, understand this: dying is not about you, the living. It is about the dying. And the dying need their loved ones. So, get out of your comfort zone and step up to the plate. Do not let your loved one believe you do not care when they leave this world.

Embracing Purpose

Purpose is what drives us forward in life. Viktor Frankl, a Jewish psychiatrist confined to a German concentration camp, observed that individuals who had something to live for, some important purpose in their lives, were more likely to make it through the unbearable experience. I believe a sense of purpose does the same for those of us experiencing grief.

When Bob and my mother died, I had been giving care for most of 22 years. During that time, my auto-immune illnesses forced me to give up my consulting practice. My reason to exist, without consciously realizing it, had become one of a caregiver. After they died and the grief set in, I had to redefine my purpose in life. Below is the process I used to find meaning in my life once again.

What do I value?

I find whatever important issue sits before me and stares me down, having a sense of my own values is critical. Why? Because our values are fundamental to whom we are as individuals, and they guide our decision-making. When we make decisions that are not consistent with our values, we end up living with regrets. For example, if we do not believe in hurting others, yet we drink, drive, and cause an accident that harms someone, we can face a life of regrets.

I know this about me: I value loyalty, honesty and compassion. My first husband and I did not share the same values, which of course, caused genuine trust problems. We all know people who have different values than we have, and we can care about them, even enjoy them.

Marrying someone with different values, however, is not easy.

The longer I knew Jack, the less I respected his values. I was planning to leave him prior to his diagnosis, but once he was diagnosed, his values became less important than my own. I knew I could not walk away from a dying man regardless of how he lived his life. That I did not like his values became irrelevant. My choice was to honor my own values. In that process, my own anger and frustration began to subside. I do not know if he healed emotionally, but I did. Staying to care for him was a choice I never regretted.

What are my hopes and dreams for the future? What have I always wanted to do?

This question can be difficult to answer for two major reasons. First, the pain of grief needs to lessen before we can focus on a new future. Second, if our loss was a spouse, half of the team is gone, which can change the plans you had made together.

My dream had always been to travel the world, but my hopes and dreams for the future changed due to my husband's death, and the diseases which forced me to give up my work. After spending so many years caring for both husbands and my mother, I had no path forward for my future. I was truly starting over. With no major responsibilities and in spite of the loss I felt, I had to find a new purpose.

Sitting alone at home, I began to write to express myself. I found a great need to be creative, a need that had not been developed in my life. Now, I can play with words on a page until they come alive and people can see and feel my world. It has become a passion.

I also love learning. If my brain is not creating, it needs to be processing, so I put myself in learning environments.

In reflecting, I was happiest when helping others, whether it was helping people in my work in sex education, helping people find jobs, or helping executives better run their companies. I knew giving to others would lessen my sadness, and be a path toward a deeper, more fulfilling destiny.

I also found the need for more interaction with others. Unchallenged, my brain drifts into worry, anxiety or meaningless internal chatter. Boredom is unhealthy. It is also a decision. You can opt to stay bored or you can decide to get involved.

What 2-3 steps did I take to create my future?

In business, we consider "steps" goals when it comes to redesigning your future. When you create your goals or steps, be specific about what you hope to achieve. Then write it down. Set up a timeline of steps to move forward, and review it regularly. But *write it down.* Written goals are more likely to be achieved than goals never committed to paper.

My focus became writing. I joined a writers group to get more feedback to hone my skills, and began taking online classes in writing. After completing those classes, I took writing classes through the local university, improving my skills even more. So my first goal was to write and publish.

My next goal was to engage in intellectual stimulation, so I joined OLLI (Osher Lifelong Learning Institute), a program for retired citizens designed to keep people physically and socially active, and mentally challenged. The intellectual stimulation kept my mind active in positive ways, warding off boredom and much of the sadness of grief.

After two years, it was time to reevaluate my living situation. Since I lived 30 miles from my friends, my third goal was to move back to Orange County to create a greater sense of community. I needed to be close to people who supported me in developing my skills, and who believed in the new life I chose to create.

The fourth goal was to turn my attention to helping others. I currently coach several young people around work and life issues. I also invited my nephew to live with me, so he could afford to attend college, a dream of his for some time. Consequently, I have fun watching him achieve his goals. For me, helping others is a profoundly satisfying experience.

What did I need to help me get there? Who helped me move forward?

When you answer this question, it is helpful to be specific. What resources, skills, or connections do you need to move you toward your new purpose? In your group of friends and family, who might be willing to help and in what ways do you need their help? Be clear about your needs and communicate them.

The OLLI program was perfect to address my writing and intellectual goals. My friends at the university have been an amazing source of support for my writing. I have turned to business friends for coaching on how to market my book. Other writers have taken their time to read, edit and provide me with feedback to improve my book. I am so thankful to so many people. This eclectic group of friends helped me launch my memoir, and have been a wonderful source of intellectual stimulation.

What you need to remember is that we all need resources to achieve our goals. So know what you need, and ask for help if you need it. Like death, repurposing life is often done best in a community.

What could hinder my progress, if any? What is the best way to manage this hindrance?

Every goal will typically have hindrances to address. My philosophy is if there is something in the way of an important goal, find an acceptable path around it. Think ahead and make plans to address any hindrances you might encounter. You will be prepared if they arise.

I had hindrances get in the way, such as getting very sick and unable to keep the deadlines for listing the house, etc., but those timelines can be altered when necessary. Timelines were also off on some of the publishing efforts, but those too, fell into a natural order. As long as my goals moved forward, timelines could be adjusted as necessary.

It is important to consider the impact of hindrances you may encounter. If finances are an issue, work within your financial limits to achieve your goals. If the issues are objections from family and friends, try to help them understand how important your goals are to you. If your goals are attainable, and within your financial boundaries, move forward! This life is yours. You have the right to create meaning in your life.

How will I celebrate moving forward while still honoring my past?

Every day I honor the special relationships I had with my husband, Bob, and my mother, Elma. I appreciate what they taught me, how they supported me, and the love they gave me. Truth is, I know—even when I did not want to move on—they were on some other plane of existence cheering me on. This book was written not just about my husband and mother, but in honor of both of them.

I celebrate my future, too. Each successful step in the writing and publishing process is a reason to celebrate. And each successful step builds motivation, supporting the belief that motivation is series of small successes. Celebrating success creates more success.

Stop and acknowledge what you have accomplished. It is not necessary to have a huge party or a plane flying overhead with a banner, but notice your progress. Build your own momentum. And celebrate your successes with those who care about you and your future.

Final Words

First, you have traveled this path of grief with me. Thank you, and I am honored by your interest. Now, I encourage you to give this gift to yourself:

- Find your purpose. If you have an existing purpose, develop it further. If you need to repurpose or define a new one, make the decision to commit to it.
- Determine the steps or goals that will carry you toward your purpose. They do not have to be perfect, but they need to clearly reflect your intentions and a timeline.
- Identify what you need to help you achieve these steps, then decide how to get what you need. Do not give up.
- Identify anything that can get in the way of moving forward. Next, decide how you will manage issues that could prevent you from moving forward.
- Now, celebrate your successes.

Remember, how you respond to loss is a decision, not a result of circumstances. Allow yourself to grieve, but decide to move forward in a way that gives life value. Finding the meaning in your life is another way of honoring your loved ones.

As Viktor Frankl wrote, "Death itself is what makes life meaningful."

I hope this book helped you learn how death can add meaning to your life.

Wishing you peace,

Jeanette

Made in the USA
San Bernardino, CA
21 October 2017